MW01277562

copyright @ 1998 by Missionary Oblates of Mary Immaculate
ISBN 0-9665255-0-7

REV. A. M. GARIN, O.M.I.
Born in France, May 7, 1822
Died in Lowell, February 16, 1895

HE WENT ABOUT DOING GOOD
ERECTED BY THE PEOPLE OF LOWELL

Gaston Carriere, OMI

THE MAN LOWELL REMEMBERED

Andre-Marie Garin, OMI
1822-1895

His Missionary Life
His Legacy to Lowell

A Tribute of gratitude from the Oblates of Lowell

Translation and editing
Lucien A. Sawyer, OMI

PREFACE

The statue of a priest by the Catholic church of Nuestra Senora del Carmen on Merrimack Street in Lowell has been there for so long that many residents hardly take notice of it. Or if they do, they may think it only natural that a monument to an early pastor would be erected there by grateful parishioners some time in the last century.

But if anyone takes the time to scan the bottom line on the base of this statue, it reads: "Erected by the people of Lowell." This serves as a reminder that the venture to erect this statue in 1896 was a civic one. It involved everyone in the city, regardless of religious persuasions. The events that led to that occasion are the substance of this book.

In 1964 Father Gaston Carriere OMI, a Canadian historian, researched and put in writing the life of Father Andre Garin OMI, the man who is represented in this statue. The book: "L'inoubliable Fondateur" was written in French. It brought to life for a new generation the extraordinary accomplishments of a dedicated priest, who died in Lowell in 1895, after contributing so much to the city.

The present volume is a translation of Father Carriere's book so that it can be shared with a wider audience of readers. People interested in the history of Lowell will be fascinated. Everything in this translation is taken from the French original.

As translator and editor, I have occasionally rearranged the sequence of events to make the chronology easier to follow. Some incidents, particularly during Father Garin's life among the Indians of northern Canada, have been shortened to keep the story flowing. The title has been changed to: "The Man Lowell Remembered" which gives a more precise focus to Father Garin's true greatness in the last 27 years of his life. But the spirit that animates this narration is due to the talent of the original French Canadian author. The book will speak for itself.

I am grateful to my Province of the Oblates of Mary Immaculate for encouraging and supporting me in this undertaking. I am also grateful to those who made suggestions that led to the final text of this book, in particular to Mrs. Doris Karkota.

April 12, 1998   Lucien A. Sawyer OMI
                        Translator and editor.

INTRODUCTION

The name of Father Andre Marie Garin OMI will forever remain intimately linked to the religious and civil history of Lowell, Massachusetts.

However, Lowell was not the only arena of his apostolic endeavors. Parishes in many other cities and towns were also beneficiaries of his religious dedication. And prior to all this, he spent twelve years as a missionary to the Indians.

Those few sketchy lines are the basis of this story. All the facts contained herein have been historically established, since I am convinced that they are sufficient in themselves to justify this publication.

I wish to thank the following for their invaluable assistance: Rev. Louis Vannier, parish priest and archpriest of Cote-Saint-Andre, to Mr. V. Chomel, curator of the Archives, Department of the Isere, to Reverend Father Charles Sety OMI, to Mr. Jean Imbert and to Reverend Sister Paul Emile SGC.

I am especially grateful to Reverend Father Laurent Tremblay OMI, Director of Rayonnement, who graciously consented to review the manuscript and make judicious suggestions which facilitated the publication of this biography.

Gaston Carriere, OMI

August 15, 1964

Table of Contents

CHAPTER ONE
UNDER THE PROTECTION OF
"NOTRE DAME DE L'OSIER"

Andre-Marie Garin, who would one day bring the Missionary Oblates of Mary Immaculate to Lowell, Massachusetts, was born at Cote-Saint-Andre in France on May 9, 1822. He was the sixth and last child[1] of a grocery merchant, Philibert Garin, and his wife, Francoise Emptoz-Falcoz Garin.

His place of birth was once the commercial center of the Isere region[2] of France, where religion was always vital, and even at times the focus of controversy. It is still blessed with beautiful surrounding landscapes: a vast plain, rolling mountains on the horizon, and two flowing rivers, the Bievre and Valloire.[3] The area has provided the background for many painters and the inspiration for many poets.[4] The numerous educational institutions have always maintained high standards.

Many years later, Father Garin would tell how his mother revealed that she had dedicated him to the Blessed Virgin, before his birth. Her action was inspired no doubt by her great devotion to "Notre Dame de l'Osier," the "Good Lady of the Dauphine." The day after he was born, he was baptized Andre,[5] and, probably at the urging of his mother, his name was extended to include Marie. After a short elementary education in his village, Andre-Marie transferred to the parochial secondary school at the Cote-Saint-Andre as a day student.[6] His older sister would awaken him at five o'clock every morning, thus developing a lifelong habit of rising early. At vacation time, the future Oblate enjoyed praying at the Twelfth Century church of Cote-Saint-Andre, a place of worship recognized for "its breadth of concept and architectural purity, suggesting the eloquence found only in the most stately of edifices."[7]

Andre's long-time companion, Father Adolphe Tortel, observed that the Garins were devout Catholics. Their faith always took precedence over their wealth and social prestige.[8] Father Tortel also wrote that Andre was not among the most studious at the school. "With his maturing intelligence and sound judgment, had he applied himself, he could have risen to the head of his class; but he was content to be an average student. Joking about it later, Father Garin said that of all the prizes awarded by the school, the only one that he ever presented to his father was for winning a track race. But his good humor, pleasant personality, kind heart, and gentle behavior won the affection of his teachers and of his fellow students."[9]

Upon completing his formal studies, Andre decided to become a priest

1

in the Congregation of the Oblates of Mary Immaculate. During his years as a student he had learned about this religious family, and grew to respect it and its members.

At the celebration of his Golden Jubilee of religious life, Father Garin recounted a conversation with his mother about his decision to become an Oblate missionary.

"Near the end of my studies," he said, "I had to choose some form of career. I had read a great deal about the exploits of missionaries among the North American Indians. I knew that the Oblates sent a good number of their priests across the Atlantic. I was eager to join the ranks of this evangelical army, but I did not want to take the final decision before consulting with my mother.

"When a suitable occasion arose, I told her of my intention. She listened attentively, embraced me tenderly, and said: 'My son, I couldn't be happier. God be praised! I don't want to influence your choice in any way: you are and always have been free. However, I believe the moment has come to tell you of a crucial event in both our lives. It will strengthen and encourage you in your present decision.

"'Before you were born, your sister Josephine became dangerously ill and was under medical care for a long time. The doctors gave up hope of ever being able to cure her. We could only resign ourselves to the inevitable or storm heaven with our prayers. I chose the latter and made a pilgrimage to the shrine of Notre Dame de l'Osier. There, I promised that if God saved my daughter's life, I would consecrate my next child to Him: if a girl, as a religious; if a boy, as a priest. Josephine was saved and you were born!

"'I have never mentioned this to you until now; but today, I feel I must do so. Go, my son, and fulfill the promise that your mother made to Heaven!'"[10]

His mother's revelation removed all misgivings about his vocation. He understood then that his call truly came from above.

It was time to go as a pilgrim to Notre Dame de l'Osier[11] for enlightenment and counsel. At the shrine he confided his intention to Father Joseph Ambroise Vincens, master of novices for the Oblate community. The young man returned to Cote-Saint-Andre, said good-bye to his family and friends, then, with a heavy heart, left for where God was calling him.

He entered the Oblate novitiate on November 1, 1841, at Notre Dame de l'Osier. His arrival took place shortly after the revitalized program for the novices had been transferred to this shrine from Marseilles. It was now under the direction of Father Vincens. Pilgrimages of lay people to the shrine of Our Lady were now enlivened by the participation of the novices. Within the Oblate community this increase in numbers brought more family life. The novices contributed their cheerful presence and fervent piety.[12] Under Father Vincens' enlightened direction, the novitiate was filled to capacity, and was truly a school for the apostolate. One Oblate commented: "The faith, the devotion, and even the enthusiasm of the novice master were reflected in the disciples. Virtues emerged and developed in the shadow of this man. He understood human behavior and fostered strong characters in the candidates. The joys of prayer made the novitiate a true threshold of religious commitment.

"What Oblate does not fondly remember his novitiate year? Who could ever forget Notre Dame de l'Osier, the religious feasts, the mountains outlined in the distance, the long walks in the valleys or on the high ridges, the singing, the departure ceremonies for missionaries, and all the pleasures of those charming days when the religious and the apostolic life blended so well together?" [13]

Brother Garin had the good fortune of beginning his novitiate amidst an extraordinary generation of novices. He thrived within this group, many of whom became pillars of the Congregation.

He was to be tested, however, and severely so, according to his own account. During the Golden Jubilee celebration of his religious profession, Father Garin recounted the most painful and difficult trial of his life: "These testimonials in my honor have called attention to my dedication and steadfastness while facing the inevitable ordeals to which I was subjected during my life as a missionary. One must be courageous, it is true, because the ordeals are great. But these hardships are not necessarily the worst. I have suffered from cold, hunger, and thirst, but I never had to bear an ordeal as difficult and terrible as the one I experienced at the beginning of my religious life.

"This is what happened. I had been at the novitiate for a few months praying with the others, giving no thought to the outside world. One day I was called to the parlor where I was greeted by two young ladies who were childhood friends.

"I admit that before entering religious life, I too had flitted about among the flowers of my youth, and found it rather pleasant. Once I became a novice, however, I erased these flirtations from memory and gave them no further thought.

"Our conversation had a lively turn: we chatted about our homes, our parents, this person and that one, whatever occurred to us. We talked of old

3

pastimes, our reunions with friends, our amusements, and other such follies. I was enjoying this more and more, but some indefinable thing was happening to me. I was reflecting that these cousins were not stupid! When they talked of leaving, I held them back!

"One of them said in a honeyed voice, 'Have you really decided to spend your life as a religious?'

"Yes, with the grace of God.

"'You want to be a missionary among the savages! My God, I shudder at the mere thought of it!'

"Oh, it is not dangerous, Miss.

"'So young, and making so many sacrifices!'

"What else? One cannot ride to heaven in a fancy coach!

"'Won't we at least have the pleasure of seeing you in the village some day?'

"I think not, Miss, but who knows?

"'In any case, Mister Andre, remember us in your prayers! It is getting late. We have to leave now. Good-bye, Mister Andre! Good-bye!'

"I could tell those good-byes had been well rehearsed beforehand. When I returned to my room I was quite upset. I threw myself on the bed and cried. Echoing in my mind was this taunting: 'Good-bye! Mr. Andre, good-bye!' Day and night, at meditation, at prayer, I always saw the same faces, I always heard the same word, 'Good-bye!'

"Before long I became depressed and lost my joy in prayer, my love of study, my spirit of reflection. I spoke to no one of this disturbing visit, and everyone was perplexed by the sudden change in my behavior.

"Our master of novices soon suspected that a struggle was taking place within my soul, but he bided his time. One day, when I was depressed to the point of thinking of returning into the world, I decided to go to him and tell him everything.

"My friends, if ever in my life I needed courage, it was on this occasion. I sat near him and blurted out everything that was going on within me. I felt an immediate sense of release. His response was a tremendous affirmation. I shed a tear for my momentary madness, and learned a valuable lesson. I would never again be subjected to an ordeal like this one.

"The physical sufferings endured in my travels among Indian tribes paled in comparison to these moral ones. You can survive the first with laughter; you can also survive the latter, but only in tears."[14]

The ordeal that was remembered so vividly all those years must have been very painful. In Father Garin's obituary notice, Father Tortel added

4

other details about these "lady" visitors that could only come from Father Garin himself: "He could no longer contain himself. He went to the master of novices and said, 'Father, I have decided to leave. I do not believe I am able to adjust to the vocation of an Oblate missionary. I shall enter Rondeau College at Grenoble and complete my philosophical studies there.' [15]

"'I know the Rondeau,' Father Vincens replied. 'The superior, Mr. Orcel, is one of my best friends. I shall give you a letter of recommendation and you will be admitted without difficulty. But, first, my friend, let's go for a stroll in the garden. The fresh air will do us some good. Tell me what is the matter. How do you explain your change of heart? Has someone tried to influence you?'

"'Yes, Father, when I went to the parlor.'

"'Of course, I remember that Father Perrin did inform me that someone was waiting there for you.'

"'Some relatives came to see me. That visit has affected my way of thinking.'

"Once the snare was uncovered, the wise master of novices had no problem helping the young man to recognize it. A delay was agreed upon before Andre could allow everything to fall apart. Brother Garin, with his warm heart and honest nature, could eventually return to tell his novice master that the storm was over and the horizon again serene." [16]

Andre was once more his cheerful self. His novitiate year ended without further incident, and he made his religious profession on November 1, 1842.

From the novitiate of Notre Dame de l'Osier, the young religious entered the major seminary of Marseilles, which was located on Rue Rouge, [17] near the residence of the bishop. This diocesan formation center also served as a scholasticate for the Oblates. Father Charles Barthelemy Bellon was their moderator. Father Bellon had been a professor at the Seminary of Ajaccio, in Corsica. Andre immersed himself in the educational and spiritual life of the seminary along with the other scholastics. They studied theology and matured in the religious life in the presence of and under the watchful eyes of the man who became Saint Eugene de Mazenod, Bishop of Marseilles, and founder of the Oblates of Mary Immaculate.

Father Bellon's profound knowledge was surpassed only by his gentle and enlightened piety. He did not expect from others what he himself did not practice in word and deed. He became a living sermon to the seminarians and the Oblates. "In the classroom, he was a dedicated teacher. In the chapel and in the study hall, he was model of piety and regularity. As a spiritual director, he was prudent, well informed, and firm yet flexible. He was even tempered and inspired confidence. Even his conversations encouraged a fondness for prayer. He used his time wisely and studied seriously... He was organized, did many things well, and blended profound knowledge with gentle, sincere piety."[18]

Under such a teacher, Andre Garin could only become more virtuous. Having earned the confidence of the moderator, he was assigned to be the "guardian angel" of the scholastics on outings and visits to the city.

The scholastics lived as a community with the diocesan seminarians except for the evening recreation, which the Oblates spent together in the north court-yard.[19] It was there that Father Garin recruited his first candidate, and no less a candidate than the one who would later succeed the founder as superior general of the Oblates: Joseph Fabre.

Joseph was a diocesan seminarian who on occasion visited the "closed garden" to chat with Brother Garin. The young seminarian had an ardent desire to learn more about the Oblate rules. The moderator was aware of these talks, and the other scholastics didn't seem to mind. Father Garin later spoke of his handing out the "forbidden fruit" (the book of Oblate Rules which at the time could not be shared with strangers) to Mister Fabre. "I gave him my book to read and study. And whenever someone knocked at his door, he would slide the book under his pillow." In the twilight of his life, Father Garin was able to say, "This memory is now way in the past, but everything is still fresh in my heart, and I always get emotional when I speak of it."[20]

The grace of God continued its work in the young Fabre. One morning, the seminarians whispered among themselves that he was seen leaving the premises wearing a cassock. In fact, on the previous evening, Bishop de Mazenod, fully aware of what was going on, had permitted Father Bellon to invest the seminarian with the Oblate religious habit. Brother Garin, his sponsor, was at his side. The postulant left on the next day for the novitiate of Notre Dame de l'Osier.[21]

Brother Garin became the hundredth member of the Oblate Congregation when he pronounced his perpetual vows on November 1, 1843. He had been ordained a subdeacon by Bishop de Mazenod in August 1843.

At that time, several seminarians from Ireland were coming to the scholasticate at Marseilles to complete their theological studies. It was decided that Brother Garin would assist Fathers William Daly and Casimir Aubert in their effort to establish the first Oblate foundation in the British Isles.

Bishop de Mazenod regretted that Brother Garin was too young, according to canon law, for the priesthood. However the founder conferred the diaconate, which was permissible, the following June. Right after this ordination, the previous assignment was countermanded, and instead of leaving for County Cork, Brother Garin was sent to Canada.[22]

CHAPTER TWO
ARRIVAL IN CANADA

Ireland's loss was Canada's gain. Brother Garin visited the sanctuary of Notre Dame de la Garde in Marseilles, as was the custom, before his departure for North America at the end of June 1844. He left on the sailing ship Orena, accompanied by Fathers Pierre Aubert and Joseph Guigues, the future Bishop of Ottawa.[1]

Their voyage took about two months, with 35 days spent at sea. When they reached Longueuil, in Quebec, their Oblate brothers welcomed them with genuine affection and joy.

The Canadian community had almost doubled during the three years since its foundation in Montreal.[2] Six candidates from the diocese of Montreal joined the seven Oblates from France, forming a community of thirteen members, not counting the lay Brothers.

Besides their Houses at Longueuil and Bytown (later renamed Ottawa), the Oblates had recently accepted the missions of James Bay, St. Maurice, the Saguenay region and the North Coast of the St. Lawrence. Brother Garin would soon find an outlet for his zeal.

Andre continued his theological studies tutored by the strict and pious Father Jean-François Allard, future vicar apostolic of South Africa. While at Longueuil, the young deacon also formed a lifelong friendship with Brother Alexandre Tache, who would become the first archbishop of St. Boniface.

Brother Garin was appointed assistant bursar of the community shortly after his arrival at Longueuil. He was being prepared for future responsibilities.[3] The Oblates at Longueuil were delighted to have a new scholastic who would soon be ordained to the priesthood.

Oblate Father Adrien Telmon and Mother Marie-Rose, foundress of the Sisters of the Holy Names of Jesus and Mary, rejoiced even more, for another reason. Since October 1842, Father Jean-Baptiste Honorat, the Oblate superior in Canada, had been writing to Bishop de Mazenod commenting on the lack of religious educators for the young women in the countryside. The Canadian missionary believed that the French Sisters of the Holy Names of Jesus and Mary, founded by Father Francois de Paule Tempier, would do wonders in the New World. But even after long negotiations, these sisters remained unwilling to cross the Atlantic Ocean.

Father Telmon resorted to founding a similar community in Canada with the help of Eulalie Durocher, later Mother Marie-Rose. Since religious directives were necessary, Father Telmon wanted the Canadian community to follow the same rules as the French sisters. Brother Garin had been entrusted with the responsibility of delivering the precious rule book to the Canadian nuns. The sisters of Longueuil accepted the volume and kissed it with deep and loving respect.[4] Father Allard, Father Telmon's successor, was very pleased with the acquisition. The Sisters who had already adopted a religious garb, were eager to accept all the practices and customs of the sisters in Marseilles.[5]

Brother Garin also brought a doll dressed in the habit of the French sisters. It would serve as a model and an exact dress pattern for the Canadian nuns. The little family of Longueuil hosted a celebration in Andre's honor to show their appreciation for this precious gift. The sisters examined and admired the doll and called it "Soeur Bienvenue" (Sister Welcome).[6] "Soeur Bienvenue" still resides at the Hall of Remembrances, in the mother house of the nuns, and "time has faded neither its face nor its habit." [7] Brother Garin apparently was considered an envoy of God at the convent. In return, he was delighted to share with the sisters the circumstance of his own vocation.

* * *

Andre-Marie completed his theological studies at Longueuil. He was ordained to the priesthood by Bishop Ignace Bourget of Montreal in the Longueuil parish church on April 27, 1845.[8] During the previous year, the saintly bishop had been so impressed with Brother Garin's personality at their first meeting that he wrote Bishop de Mazenod, on October 10, 1844, about "the modesty and serious demeanor" of this young religious.[9]

As a priest, Father Garin could now devote himself entirely to the apostolate. He did so with the ardent zeal that marked the rest of his life. In May, a few days after his ordination, he left with Father Nicolas Laverlochere for the difficult missions of Temiscamingue, Abitibi, and Great Lake in northern Quebec.

During a period of 13 years (1844-1857) Father Garin traveled extensively as a missionary to the Indians of the Canadian North as far as James Bay, and as far East as the outer bank of the Gulf of St. Lawrence.

CHAPTER THREE
IN THE JAMES BAY MISSIONS

A few days after his ordination to the priesthood, in 1845, Father Garin traveled North with Father Nicolas Laverlochere towards Temiscamingue, Abitibi, and Great Victoria Lake. During the long canoe trips, from May to September, the young missionary began to learn the elements of the language spoken by the local Indians. He also found occasions to polish his English, a language in which he would become remarkably fluent in the years to come. Andre's tactful and pleasant personality made him a good companion for Father Laverlochere. The Indians and the employees of the Hudson's Bay Company soon accepted him as a worthy associate.[1]

Before undertaking such a journey, the missionaries always paid a visit to a special shrine dedicated to the Blessed Virgin. In a letter to a friend, Father Garin described this shrine and its significance: "In the midst of our beautiful city of Montreal, on the banks of the majestic St. Lawrence River, one can see a shrine to Mary. This shrine was built as an expression of devotion by the first French colonists who came here to develop the land.[2] It was called Notre Dame de Bonsecours. These hardy pioneers were on a strange continent, always on guard against attacks from hostile natives and exposed to countless dangers in their daily explorations. They traveled in frail bark canoes on swift rivers which narrowed into the most perilous rapids imaginable. These intrepid "voyageurs" could not have conceived a more praiseworthy and blessed project. They erected an altar of thanksgiving in this New France, to the one who had obtained so many blessings for them, and who was considered by their traditional faith as the help of all Christians.

"Every Spring, as soon as the ice has left the surface of our broad rivers, the missionary, before undertaking the distant journey to his people, never fails to visit this revered shrine of Our Lady. He needs so much help and protection for himself and for the faithful Indians whom he will see again after a long absence! He can then be on his way, confident that this loving Mother will protect him from all harm and bestow her plentiful blessings upon all his undertakings."[3]

Father Laverlochere and his new companion left Montreal on May 6, 1845, after visiting the shrine. They headed for Lac-des-Deux-Montagnes where they outfitted the canoe and hired seven men as oarsmen and guides. Their journey began, and proceeded with the anticipated hardships until they reached the foot of the three-mile rapids at Eveille. Danger lurked here.

In order to negotiate the turbulent waters more easily, the travelers unloaded half of their equipment at the foot of the rapids. Father Garin canoed up the river to the other end while Father Laverlochere stayed behind to guard their belongings. Three hours went by. The older missionary began to worry about his companions. After some delay the men suddenly emerged from the woods, soaked to the skin, but without Father Garin. Their canoe had been caught in the swirling rapids, floundered against a stump, and split in two. Their only recourse in this situation was to send a few men back to Fort-des-Allumettes, 125 miles downstream, to purchase another long canoe.

In the meantime, Father Garin was stranded on the opposite bank of the river for thirty hours, without fire or food, and without knowing the fate of his companions. This was his initiation into the perils of a missionary's life!

Father Laverlochere later wrote: "My young colleague believed that we had all drowned, and resigned himself to his fate, with no other recourse than Divine Providence. It was only during the second evening that he happened to come upon a storage boot that contained a loaf of bread. Our Indian cook from Lac-des-Deux-Montagnes had apparently stashed the bread in there to keep it fresh. Later, when we eventually found each other, the joy of our reunion made all hardships vanish."[4]

The journey moved on, with many consolations. At every outpost they preached to many Indians, and performed numerous baptisms. They often accepted the hospitality and encouragement of English agents of the Hudson's Bay Trading Company. Father Laverlochere, in a letter to his bishop, described their departure from Abitibi: "Our departure was such a solemn occasion that it astounded a group of Protestants who had recently arrived from Moose Factory. Try to imagine, my dear bishop, the sight of more than 300 Indians, many of them not yet full believers, kneeling along the water's edge. The priest is standing in his canoe, lifting his hands to Heaven, and praying with tear-filled eyes to the Father of Mercy for a blessing upon this portion of His inheritance. That was the scene at Abitibi."[5]

The response of the newly converted Indians made all their efforts worth while. Father Garin's first missionary voyage was brimming over with distress and hardships, but it provided the young Oblate with valuable and grace filled experiences. He ended his report to Father Guigues, his provincial, with these words: "Although I was happy in the midst of Indian country, I now willingly take the road back to Longueuil."[6]

Following his first missionary trek, he spent some time with the Sulpicians at Oka. These clerics offered him friendly hospitality and provided him with the opportunity to immerse himself relentlessly in the study of the predominant Indian language. At the end he emerged with a complete mastery of the idiom.[7]

His introduction to the work of a missionary was now complete. Father Andre returned several times to these regions. On his second trip, he and Father Laverlochere intended to reach as far north as Moose Factory. The journey of 2,000 miles did not intimidate them. They set their sight on that distant outpost, come what may.

Father Laverlochere left Quebec on May 8, 1847. On the 10th he departed from Montreal and headed for Lac-des-Deux-Montagnes, where a crew awaited him. In a letter to Father Jean-Claude Baveux on August 15, 1847, he wrote: "For the second time, the amiable Father Garin was chosen to accompany me. On this long trip he will serve as English interpreter."[8] Later that year, Father Garin shared the honor of being one of the first two Oblates ever to reach Moose Factory.

We have possible evidence that Father Garin served as God's instrument to open this outpost to Catholic evangelization. He refers to this subsequently in a letter dated January 15, 1853. "A gentleman from the honorable Hudson's Bay Company, traveling through our area had accepted our invitation to dinner. The agent was astonished that the Oblates had not extended their excursions as far as the shores of Hudson Bay where many tribes had never heard of the Gospel. When I mentioned the presence of Weslyan ministers, he merely shrugged his shoulders.

"As a result," Father Garin continues, "I informed the ecclesiastical authorities about this conversation. The governor of the company was approached for authorization to travel to Hudson Bay. Permission was granted; Father Laverlochere and I undertook the journey."[9]

After their first stop at Abitibi, the two Oblates headed north with a Hudson's Bay Company official and his family, along with some thirty Indians. During the long trip, the missionaries found time to teach and hear confessions. Sundays were special for the priests "who offered the Divine Victim in nature's own temple under the vault of Heaven, 7,500 miles from their homeland and 750 miles from the closest civilization, along the banks of a vast lake. The silence was total in this setting of forests as ancient as the world, where the worshipers were mainly a few Indians who, a short time ago, had been superstitious and ferocious but were now docile and pious."[10] Many challenges awaited them! At the end of Abitibi Lake, "which may be 60 miles wide and some 450 miles in circumference," they steered into the lake's outlet river towards James Bay. "It would be no more than 250 miles in a straight line to the Bay, but the journey by canoe required a course through 375 winding and arduous miles with 28 muddy portages, some of which were more than 2 miles long." The turbulent waters covered rocks lurking at times a mere two inches below the surface. The alerts from the navigator were constant. Add to this the oppressive heat and the mortal enemies of missionaries -- mosquitoes and black flies. As if this were not enough, they experienced an abrupt drop in temperature, followed by a heavy snow storm. Gloves were now needed for paddling. When they awoke in the morning their tent was often stiff and frozen. As they neared the Bay enormous ice floes lined the shore.

Finally, at about nine o'clock, on the morning of June 19, the priests caught sight of Moose Factory. The beautiful lines of the fort gave it the appearance of a village.

After receiving many amenities from the chief agent of the post the Oblates provided the Sacraments for the many newly converted Indians who welcomed them with many demonstrations.[11] The missionaries had even planned to continue their route up to Fort Albany, 250 miles beyond Moose Factory, when a Mrs. Corcoran, the wife of the Commander of Fort Albany arrived with her son.

She told the Fathers that the Indians had left that area. She added that her husband, a devout Catholic, would soon be joining them. In fact her husband did arrive four days later and was overjoyed at seeing the Catholic priests. He fell at their feet and thanked God for sending them. It was the answer to thirty years of prayer.

Father Laverlochere added, "Since Father Garin was fluent in English, he ministered to this worthy family. This was the only language they spoke, except for the mother." The gracious lady was familiar with all the idioms of the James Bay Indians, and she was later of great assistance to the missionaries in the translation of devotional books.

Two days after Mr. Corcoran's arrival from Albany, Father Garin baptized Mrs. Corcoran and their 22 year old daughter; their son had previously been christened in Montreal. In early July the missionaries headed for home, their hearts content with the many favors that God's Providence had sent their way.

The door to Catholic missions at James Bay was now open. The fruits of that first visit could be enjoyed but further cultivation and harvesting would demand enormous sacrifices. The way was now mapped out, and missionaries would return every year, until the time arrived to establish a permanent residence on the frigid shores of the ominous Bay.[12]

* * *

Such was Father Garin's magnificent work in the difficult James Bay mission. He shrank from no sacrifice that was necessary for his apostolic labors. He had mastered the Indian language so well, especially during his prolonged stay with the Sulpicians, that he could compose books in the Cree Indian language. From Lac-des-Deux-Montagnes, he wrote with obvious delight on December 10, 1853, "You will learn with the greatest pleasure that in all likelihood we shall soon print a book for our Fort Albany Indians."[13] The Society for the Propagation of the Faith, in Montreal, donated a substantial amount for the printing of this work.[14]

In 1854 Louis Perreault of Montreal, published a 94-page Catechism, Book of Prayers and Hymns for the Use of the Indians of Albany. This was written in collaboration with Father Laverlochere. In 1856, the Perreault House produced Father Garin's 63-page Way of the Cross and Other Prayers for the Use of the Indians of Albany, Severn, Martin's Falls, and in 1858, the 120-page Sermons of Bishop Baraga Translated From the 'Otcipwe' Into 'Maskgon'.

Thanks to this little portable library prepared for them through Father Garin's zeal and competence, the Indians could learn about their Faith not only while the missionaries were present, but throughout the entire year.[15]

The young priest earned the admiration and the trust of his superiors. When a project for the establishment of an apostolic prefecture for that territory arose in 1870, Father Garin's name was among the candidates for the position of bishop.[16]

12th Century Church - La Cote St.-Andre
(France)

Notre-Dame de l'Osier
(France)

Typical Family visited by Oblate Missionaries
in Northern Canada

CHAPTER FOUR
FROM MONTREAL TO THE GULF OF THE
ST. LAWRENCE

In 1847 we find Father Garin ministering in the urban setting of Montreal. That year, a potentially dangerous situation arose. Thousands of poor Irish immigrants were being ravaged by a typhus epidemic. There was an urgent need for courageous priests. Father Garin, with his fluency in English, was chosen to assist. He worked night and day with Fathers Damase Dandurand, Michael Molloy, Eusebe Durocher, and Medard Bourassa, alongside local diocesan clergy. Fortunately he was spared from the effects of this grim scourge that ended the lives of Fathers Dandurand and Molloy[1]

After this episode, Father Garin devoted himself for a time to parish ministry at St. Marie's, a temporary chapel outside of Montreal. This was an extension of St. Peter's parish in the city. He heard confessions several days a week and preached frequently.

The young priest was a model for his times. He was gentlemanly, with impressive and engaging manners. In the pulpit, his natural gestures, his clear explanations, his rich and resonant voice endeared him to the people. They viewed him already as a master of the homily. He even reached out to negligent and stubborn hearts with a gentle use of irony. This eloquent priest was a delight to see and hear.[2]

* * * * * * *

Father Garin once said that his vocation was influenced by the written accounts of Oblate missionaries. It was undoubtedly in response to his missionary aspirations that, in September of 1845, following his first mission to Lakes Temiscamingue and Abitibi, he was now assigned to the Saguenay region. He made two visits to the St. Lawrence Gulf region, once, in 1846 with Father Flavien Durocher, and again in 1850 with Father Charles Arnaud.[3]

On April 27, 1846, Father Garin left from St. Alexis on Great Bay, in the company of Father Durocher, the renowned apostle of the Montagnais Indians.[4] Two days later, their first important stop was at Tadoussac. There the Indians chided Father Durocher for not visiting them during the winter while his young companion was ministering in the lumber camps. Father Durocher explained in a letter: "As a matter of fact it was in March that

Father Garin, while enduring incredible hardships, had covered the many settlements of the lower Saguenay and various lumber camps on the St. Lawrence River. During this time, I was helping the people of Chicoutimi to fulfill their Easter duties."[5]

On the first Sunday of May, they carefully prepared a site for the celebration of Mass at Escoumains. Some twenty Indian families left their seal hunting on nearby beaches and hastened to join the group. The missionaries went on to the Ilets-de-Jeremie, where on May 5, they announced that the bishop would be coming. The Sacrament of Confirmation was about to be administered for the first time to the Montagnais tribe.[6]

The priests traveled further up the coast but returned to Islets-de-Jeremie in July. At the first sign of the outpost, the travelers hoisted their little flag. Soon the harbor banner fluttered in response from the top of its mast. Strong winds and an ebbing tide kept them a mile from the landing, but as night approached two light canoes came out to meet them. Father Garin climbed aboard one of them and Father Durocher boarded the other. They raced to see which canoe would be first to reach the shore.

The missionaries had only eleven days to prepare the Indians for the Bishop's visit. More and more Montagnais Indians arrived every day. Even some Naskapies, catechumens and neophytes, came down from their mountains. They listened with reverence to our Christian hymns, and expressed the hope that those of their fellow countrymen who were still pagan could experience the same happiness. Bishop Flavien Turgeon of Quebec arrived at Ilets-de-Jeremie on July 20th to confer the Sacrament of Confirmation, as announced to the Indians at the beginning of Summer.

"Outsiders," Father Durocher wrote later in his report,"were astonished to see these inhabitants of the forests praying from their books during worship services. They were especially surprised to learn that the primary education, received generations ago from the Jesuit pioneers, was being handed down from father to son without the help of foreign teachers. No less astonishing was that knowledge of Gregorian chant could be preserved in the same fashion by our Indians of Ilets-de-Jeremie. Father Garin had left them two copies of Credo II after a single exercise of it. Upon his return from missions in the Aval region, he hurried to bring his singers together. He intoned the Credo, and all responded in firm and confident unison."[7]

Bishop Turgeon confirmed 171 Indians during the three days of his episcopal visit, ending with a pontifical Mass on the last day. The Montagnais performed a majestic rendition of the Messe Royale. The Introit, especially, Nottauinan (Gaudeamus) was rendered flawlessly.

The two Oblate priests returned to their boats at the end of this Mass. At the end of their journey, instead of returning to the Montreal community, the fathers headed for Pointe-des-Monts,[8] where they accepted the hospitality of the lighthouse keeper and spent the winter studying the Montagnais language.

Life at Pointe-des-Monts was truly that of a hermitage. Father Garin later described their quarters when he was called upon to write an obituary of Father Durocher. "Our residence was a government lighthouse, a six-story stone tower, with two stories at our disposal. I lived there for five months in the same room with him [Father Durocher]. I can say that I knew him, admired him, and loved him. I never saw him lose a minute. He was up at four o'clock in the morning, but he let his young companion sleep until five. I was often embarrassed in our travels, above all with strangers, seeing him set aside for us the best portions of food, the most comfortable seats, and the least rugged beds."[9]

On November 7, Father Durocher wrote in a letter to Father Cazeau, the vicar general of Quebec, that Father Garin was pursuing his study of the Montagnais language with great determination.[10]

Isolation weighed heavily on young Father Garin during that winter, but his companion's kindness lightened the burden and allowed Andre to get in touch with his proficiency in languages.

The following Spring, as they were leaving for Quebec, where they had been called, the missionaries encountered life-threatening perils.

Father Garin's account follows: "On Saturday, March 19th, Father Flavien (Durocher) and I bid farewell to our good Montagnais, who were greatly saddened by our departure. Our small party consisted of a four-man crew in two birch canoes that measured 12 feet by 2. Our provisions consisted of a mere 60 pounds of biscuits and about 30 or 40 pounds of bacon. The first two days on the water were without serious incident. The first sign of trouble came on Saturday, when we had planned to reach Ilets-de-Jeremie to offer Mass there on the next day. The weather had been beautiful up to 3 o'clock in the afternoon, when our crew beached the canoes for our first meal of the day. By 4 o'clock, we were again in our canoes eager to cover the fifteen miles to Ilets-de-Jeremie.

"We had before us a nine-mile stretch across a bay that was deep and wide, but our men were hardy and the rising tide was in our favor. All went well until we were half way to the land ahead. At that point we began to encounter ice floes that forced us to make several long detours. We were hoping to avoid other ice floes and find an outlet to bring us to our destination. The more we advanced, however, the more numerous the sheets of ice. We soon realized that we would have to backtrack without delay, since the passage forward was completely blocked. We turned back quickly toward the shore we had left an hour and a half earlier.

"Despite our efforts to paddle faster, we could not outpace the approaching nightfall. To make matters worse, all our efforts were thwarted by the overpowering current of the ebbing sea. We were rapidly being drawn into the open gulf which was at least 54 miles wide at this point. The intense concentration of our Indian paddlers made it clear to us that we were in grave danger. Father Durocher and I began to recite the Ave Maris Stella and the Rosary. Those prayers had barely ended when thick darkness engulfed us from all sides. The shore had vanished completely from sight. We raised our eyes skyward in vain. Not a single star was shining to guide our course.

"In the dreadful darkness that prevailed, we could barely discern one person from another. We no longer knew where we were going nor where we were. For awhile we let our canoes drift with the currents. As we began paddling again, now more slowly and with great difficulty, we attempted to skirt the mounds of snow and half-frozen water. The blocks of ice were getting harder and threatened to capsize us. At around 9 o'clock in the evening, the canoes became motionless, pressed from all sides by the ice. We realized that two opposing currents had collided, causing the floes to crash against each other all around us. Our Indians stopped paddling and we all rocked the canoe sometimes to the right and sometimes to the left to avoid being crushed. These motions allowed the sheets of ice to slide over each other.

"For about half an hour the strenuous and very dangerous maneuvers brought sweat to our brows. Our Indians, who had maintained a gloomy silence until then, began to say: 'Fathers, what's going to become of us? The birch of our canoes cannot withstand this constant scraping much longer. My God, what's going to become of us?'

"After speaking to each other for a moment Father Durocher and I answered them: 'Let us all promise together to sing a solemn Mass in honor of St. Anne if she will deliver us from the imminent death that now threatens all of us.'

"'Yes, Fathers, we promise.'

"A moment later, the currents stopped and the ice floes ceased smashing into one another! Without hesitation, our guide told us that we must jettison our cargo to lighten the canoes and enable them to slide onto the top of the ice. We kept the Mass vestments, the chalice and four or five pounds of biscuits. Everything else was thrown overboard— rifles, shot, provisions, books, and altar stone.

"One of our Indians grasped the missal as it was about to be jettisoned. 'What! The prayer book too! No! No! If we are going to die, it shall perish only when we do!'

"After we had lightened the canoe, our guide instructed each of us to lace a snowshoe on one foot, and with that foot press gently against the ice. The other foot remained in the canoe. In this manner we were able to free ourselves from the sharp ice that could have pierced the bark at any moment.

"In the meantime, the other canoe was ahead of us and equally in danger. We had to help them, no matter the cost. Our guide tested the ice next to us with his paddle. When he felt that it was solid and capable of supporting him, he jumped onto it. He tied several belts together, threw one end of this tether to his companion in the other canoe, and drew the others towards us.

"At that moment, our guide had a providential and divine inspiration! 'Fathers, we must camp here on this ice for the night.'

"Never were we more promptly and more perfectly obedient. Without another word, we slid onto the ice and lay next to each other on our seal skins. The floe that served as our bed must have been about 20 square feet. It was about eleven o'clock at night. Our Indians had worked unceasingly all day on only one meal. They were exhausted and in dire need of rest. But, since they had not yet recited the Rosary, they quickly knelt on the ice and we all prayed together.

"Some people might think that under these conditions it would be impossible to close one's eyes and fall asleep. They don't know the resilience of a missionary character. I fell into a deep sleep until Father Durocher awakened me around midnight. A terrible storm was brewing in the distance. We could hear the sea howling furiously and the wind seemed to want to blow us off the ice.

"One of our Indians cried out in an ominous voice: 'Fathers, we are lost!'

"We again turned to Saint Anne, beseeching her to spare our Indians for their families who might blame the impending calamity on our religion. We had barely directed our prayers to this powerful Saint when the wind died down instantly and completely. The storm had lasted scarcely more than five minutes.

"We were wide awake at the first sign of daybreak. We launched our canoes towards a distant glimpse of land. After incredible hardships, we finally reached the shore, and not a moment too soon. Minutes later the sea began to churn under the storm, hurling waves towards the sky.

"We found a secure spot in the deep woods and set up a tolerable camp. We spent the rest of the Lord's day in blessings and thanksgiving, thanking

God for the remarkable protection granted to us through the intercession of Saint Anne."[11]

Father Garin never forgot this missionary adventure and the protection that "la bonne Sainte Anne" had lavished on him at this crucial moment in his life.

* * *

Instead of returning at once to the Saguenay region, Father Garin was sent on another journey to James Bay with Father Laverlochere in 1847. The following year he remained in Montreal with his colleagues, ministering mostly to urban populations, especially at St. Alexis and St. Alphonse. Yet he still spent a considerable part of the winter going to the lumbermen in the Saguenay region. There, he willingly shared in all the undertakings and the trials of his valiant superior, Father Honorat. During the summer of 1848, he sided with unfortunate people who were in difficulty with the police concerning a land dispute that involved the church at Great Bay. He explained the incident in a letter dated July 29, 1848, to Father Cazeau, Vicar General of Quebec: "Today, all these men are prisoners and have been taken to Quebec. I don't know what is going to happen to them. Everyone here agrees with their defense of church property rights. They are following the advice of Mr. Laterriere and people who know the law.

"We briefed Bishop Turgeon while he was here, but he will be unable to return to Quebec in time to pursue this affair. I beg you, therefore, to intercede for them. Try to find bondsmen for these men who are fearful of going to prison. Among them are some of our most honest and well-to-do parishioners. They are our current and former church trustees and are all good men. In their zeal, they upheld the rights of their church and our religion. If any mistakes were made, it seems to me that they could be easily overlooked."[12]

Father Garin was always a living example of the good shepherd who defended his flock from what he considered an injustice. He would fight all his life for the rights of his congregation, but would at the same time emphasize their obligations.

* * * * *

His final missionary journey to the St. Lawrence Gulf region was in 1850 with Father Arnaud, who was to become the great missionary of the North Coast. Andre wrote that his companion "was finding the site more poetical than the swamps and mosquitoes of Hudson Bay," which had been Father Arnaud's introduction to the missionary life.

Father Garin anticipated that the first ceremony to be performed on this expedition would be Father Arnaud's "baptism of fire", as this was his first voyage among the Coastal Montagnais. Father Arnaud would later be named by the Indians "Ka Uashkamuesht," the "tenor voice" or the "clear voice." The young missionary would retain this title all his life.

It was also at this mission that the Indians adopted Father Arnaud as one of their own. They paid him a great honor with these simple words: "Nota, tshi usham miloasho miam ilno": " Father, you are as beautiful as an Indian." The priest was very proud of the compliment.[13] It would not be unseemly to presume that Father Garin's early influence on young Father Arnaud during this first voyage to the Coast was in great measure responsible for the admirable zeal that marked the latter's career. A previous mission to James Bay in 1849 by Father Arnaud had left him somewhat disillusioned.

Father Garin desired to head further north. He was ready to span the world, no matter the hardships and sacrifices. His ambition was as far-reaching as that of Father Arnaud, his companion of the 1850 trip, who was dreaming of a possible Oblate mission to Greenland.

During the construction of Immaculate Conception church in Lowell, the former missionary thought of giving a series of conferences entitled "Twelve Years Among the Indians."[14] Unfortunately, these conferences were never given, and we have been deprived of what could have been a valuable source of information.

* * * * * * *

Following his last mission to the Saguenay, Father Garin joined the Montreal community of the Oblates and participated once more in their ministry.

In his free moments, he was able to observe at first hand the construction of the magnificent St. Peter's Church of Montreal, which had been entrusted to the Oblates in 1851.[15] He was thus preparing himself for future tasks in Lowell.

Much of the ministry of the Oblate community in Montreal was devoted to retreats and missions. Father Garin did his share of preaching during the winters of 1849-1850 and 1850-1851. In November of 1849, he teamed up with Father Lucien Lagier at the church of St. Roch, in the town of Assumption. This was the beginning of a partnership that would last through numerous apostolic endeavors, the most famous of which was to be in Lowell, in the Spring of 1868.

Many of his successes were recorded in the house diary called the "Codex Historicus." He preached a mission at St. Timothy's Church in 1850 with remarkable results. In the Cathedral of Montreal, more than 900 men approached the Communion rail on Christmas day. At the end of a retreat at St. Hyacinthe, in 1851, 1,100 Communions were recorded. An Oblate historian in Montreal noted that serious dissensions which had existed in that last parish disappeared after the mission.[16]

The 1851 mission in Sorel also yielded exceptional results. Fathers Lucien Lagier, Edouard Chevalier, Pierre-Julien Amisse, and Andre-Marie Garin, opened their three-week retreat on the eve of Epiphany. Many of the parishioners, according to the Oblate historian, avidly pursued worldly gains but sadly neglected the spiritual requirements for a good life. Moreover, the demon of discord was afoot in the parish. As soon as the mission was underway, however, the church began to fill with worshipers who responded to the eloquence of the preachers. Strangers were attracted who had rarely or ever seen the inside of the church. Women brought their children and were not reluctant to walk ten to twelve miles in the snow for a share in the blessings of the Lord's Mercy. More than 4,000 people were present to renew their baptismal promises, and more than 1,200 men received Communion.[17] The Oblate missionaries achieved the same success with missions given at Berthier,[18] and at Lanoraie during March.[19]

Because of the bonds of friendship that had been forged with Bishop Tache in the early days at Longueuil, Father Garin was asked to accompany the bishop on a tour of France. The two Oblates left for Europe on November 21, 1856. Their task was to spend the winter preaching in favor of the Pontifical Society for the Propagation of the Faith. They accomplished this by sharing various dioceses of France. Each of them turned out to be as successful as Fathers Laverlochere and Jean-Claude Leonard Baveux had been previously.[20] The outcome was certainly momentous. It was comparable to the results achieved by Father Baveux on a preaching tour of 1847, when seventy-two new recruits for the Oblates were enlisted.[21]

CHAPTER FIVE
PLATTSBURGH AND BUFFALO

The greater part of Father Andre-Marie Garin's life, and the most active, was spent in the United States. His first ministry there was perhaps in 1854. He had barely returned from James Bay, on September 7, when he was sent to give support to Fathers Lagier, Rouisse and Royer who had opened a mission at Corbeau[1], New York, on September 3rd.

He later served with fellow Oblates in St. Joseph parish in Burlington, Vermont, from September 21 to November 11, 1856. Traces of his dynamic zeal were recorded in Vergennes,[2] and Williston on September 21 and October 15, 1856, as well as in Milton on November 11. This was followed by his preaching tour in Europe, in the company of Bishop Tache. Upon his return, in October 1857, he was assigned to Plattsburgh, New York for a term of five years.

Father Garin arrived in that city at a moment of crisis, the parish was badly in need of a peacemaker. To understand the situation we must recall the facts that led to this impasse. The Oblates had been invited to take over the parish of Plattsburgh in 1853. Their provincial council responded favorably to this request July 8, and an agreement was signed on July 28 between Bishop John McCloskey and the provincial, Father Jacques Santoni. Father Jean-Pierre Bernard became the first superior of the new community. Father Bernard, who had supervised the construction of St. Peter's in Montreal, immediately started the construction of a church, 155 by 66 feet in dimension. It was based on the plans of the Canadian architect Victor Bourgeault. Bishop Joseph-Eugene Bruno Guigues OMI blessed the church on June 29, 1855. The rectory had been built during the previous year, 1854.

At Father Garin's arrival, the parish register counted 1263 parishioners, in 200 families, living in the town. An additional 1680 parishioners, in about 400 families, resided within a radius of fifteen to sixteen miles in the countryside. Many of these parishioners belonged to the Temperance Society and received the sacraments frequently.

Beneath this peaceful appearance, there was trouble brewing. The Oblate community was at odds with the trustees. Mutual misunderstandings and suspicions were rampant, probably due to absolute positions taken by both sides. Stubbornness aggravated the uneasiness. Father Garin appeared on the scene as a calm leader without arrogance, who knew how to listen, concede, inspire confidence, smile, and above all, reach out amicably to everyone. The petty hatreds calmed down, anger faded and the most disparate elements melded together. Within a few months Father Garin succeeded in bringing unity and peace to this parish.

The church construction was easily completed in this atmosphere of peace and harmony. The Oblate provincial was manifestly pleased. In 1858, he wrote to Bishop McCloskey of Albany, "On my way to Quebec...I stopped in Plattsburgh to visit the Reverend Fathers who live there. I observed with pleasure how the community of French Canadians fondly remembered the good effects of your pastoral visit last year. Unity and tranquility have replaced strife...The priests are busy with the church windows and are redoing the sacristy. I wish them well in both tasks."[3]

The construction was completely finished, and the steeple was in place, by 1861.[4] Father Garin could now undertake other equally urgent tasks.

The superior and the priests in Plattsburgh were distressed that some children were not attending school or were attending classes that were under Protestant influence. As a result, Father Garin planned to establish a parochial school.

Bishop Guigues approved this project, as he recorded in his Act of Visitation dated April 29, 1858: "We authorize the erection of a boarding school near the church. Before taking any steps in this direction, however, we need a response from the bishop of Albany."[5]

In a letter to the provincial dated May 23, 1858, the bishop of Albany gave his approval to the foundation of a boarding school at Plattsburgh, to be staffed by the Gray Nuns of Ottawa. This was in response to a letter received earlier that month from Bishop Guigues who had described the project in these terms: "to construct a spacious building for the education of young people, to seek out a community of religious women for this instruction, and to provide guidance for the young boarders who would come there." The task could prove difficult in a young and impoverished town like Plattsburgh. Yet, it seemed feasible. Even a certain number of Protestants offered to back this project, while the Canadian and Irish Catholics would deem it their duty to subscribe.[6]

Father Garin received Bishop McCloskey's reply with great joy, and Bishop Guigues urged him on to a speedy realization. For some unknown reason, however, the project was delayed. It was not until March 12, 1860, that Father Garin could finally report to Bishop Guigues that the contract for the convent had been let out for $7,500.[7] Bishop Guigues was invited to Plattsburgh for ceremonies on May 20, which climaxed with the blessing of the corner stone. The new brick structure would measure 45 by 60 feet. Father Garin had already been to Ottawa on November 28, 1859, to invite the Gray Nuns to assume direction of the school. He was thoughtful enough to bring along detailed plans of the building under construction.[8]

The work proceeded briskly and Father Garin believed that the house could be opened for All Saints' Day. But much depended on the reply from the bishop of Albany concerning the Gray Nuns of Ottawa.[9]

The Codex Historicus of the Oblate residence records that the Gray Nuns, eight in number, arrived on November 3, 1860. While the boarding school was intended for young ladies, the Sisters would also direct a day school for the young Canadian and Irish girls of the parish. Also, two of the nuns looked after the sick among the poor while awaiting the hand of Providence to establish a hospital.[10]

The blessing of the convent school took place on November 4, and classes started on November 12. The little town of Plattsburgh was now endowed with an excellent academy for young women.

This appears to have been Father Garin's choice task. The sisters had a grand reception on that first Sunday after their arrival! They were welcomed at the church door by the first trustee. In the afternoon there was a solemn procession leading to the blessing of the new convent.

The nuns noted that Father Garin was greatly moved as he celebrated Mass for First Communion at the convent on December 23, 1860, especially at communion time. Many of the participants responded with tears of their own.

The annals of the Sisters of Plattsburgh frequently report that Father visited the nuns, encouraged them, assisted at examination time, preached, even brought books and world globes for the classes.

The question of a similar school for boys was posed to the provincial council of September 12, 1861, but it seems that nothing could be done during the remaining time of Father Garin's tenure as superior.

He did not, however, limit his ministry in Plattsburgh exclusively to the French-speaking parishioners of St. Peter's Church. He devoted himself equally to the English-speaking congregation of St. John the Baptist Parish in the same town.

With the acceptance of ministry to the Canadians living in Plattsburgh, the Oblate provincial council envisioned a time when that Congregation would minister to the whole town, including the Irish Catholics. This became a reality in the summer of 1860.

A chapel at Cadyville was attached to St. John the Baptist parish. When Father Richard Moloney was asked to look after this mission he also became pastor at the mother parish.[11] The Oblates worked there until August 15, 1878, without requiring any particular intervention from the pastor of St. Peter's.

As superior of Plattsburgh, Father Garin relied mostly on members of his community for the important missions of Redford and Dannemora. He must have kept an eye though on the task begun in 1858 by Father Claude Sallaz in the construction, and later in the expansion (1861-1862), of the chapel at the Dannemora State Prison. He was constantly reaching out to smaller towns throughout the area. Local announcements note his activities at Port Jackson, Barthonville, Salmon River, Schyler Falls, Morissonville, Pointe-aux-Roches, Wood Mill, Neap City, West Beakmantown, State Road, Cumberland Head, Creek, Rand Hill, Turnpike, Beakmantown, Chazy and West Chazy. It amounted to a small diocese!

At one point Father Garin turned his interest towards St. Jean-Baptiste Parish of Keeseville. On December 17, 1857, he informed the provincial that the pastor of Keeseville was leaving his parish and perhaps this departure could lead to a new post for the Oblates. He believed that with three priests on his staff, the Plattsburgh community could handle this mission which would involve only one visit every third week.[12] He wrote again in January 1858 that the people of Keeseville felt neglected and were imploring the Oblates for help. The bishop of Albany would likely anticipate some loss of Faith among the people.

Father Garin's intuition about the bishop was correct. On May 23, Bishop McCloskey wrote to the provincial begging him to serve Keeseville. The provincial had to refuse, regretfully, because a policy had been established at the last General Chapter to lessen rather than increase the number of small residences requiring only two or even three Oblates.[13]

Father Garin, as superior, had to deal with the extremely difficult situation for the Oblates in Burlington, since it involved having to gradually leave the parish in that city and the numerous missions which depended upon it. Father Garin was asked to mediate in a manner that would respect justice and minimize the hurt to the "good bishop of Burlington."[14]

In brief, Father Garin's years as superior at Plattsburgh were not marked by sensational events, yet he left an indelible memory with his flock. More than thirty years after his departure, the parish unanimously expressed their heartfelt sorrow and condolences to the Oblate priests at the news of his death .[15]

* * *

Father Garin left for his next assignment in Buffalo on September 24, 1862. Here again he was called upon to be a conciliator. The situation was more sensitive than the trouble in Plattsburgh because this time the predicament involved the Oblate priests with the diocesan authorities.

What follows is the sequence of events that led to this impasse.

The first group of Oblates had come to Buffalo on July 26, 1850. Less than a month later, they returned to Montreal on August 16, after a series of misunderstandings. While on a canonical visit to Canada in July of 1851, Father Tempier, the assistant general, traveled to Buffalo to meet with the bishop. There, he signed an agreement whereby the Oblates would assume responsibility for a major seminary, a college, and a public chapel. Father Edouard Chevalier led a new Oblate contingent to Buffalo in mid-August.

The beginnings were deplorable. The college and seminary projects had to be abandoned. The only success was the construction of a magnificent church dedicated to the Holy Angels. But even there, financial straights made it seem more than once that the project wasn't worth the effort to continue.

Father Chevalier was recalled from Buffalo at the beginning of November 1862 because of new dissensions with the bishop. Father Garin was sent as a replacement. It was not, as we can surmise, the best of times.

On October 25, 1862, Bishop Guigues informed Bishop Timon of the new superior's arrival. He introduced Father Garin as a peacemaker and one who was experienced in business matters. If an amicable solution could be reached with the bishop, as anticipated, then the provincial promised to ask the general administration to send two English-speaking Oblates for parish missions. He was sure there would be no problem if the bishop agreed.[16]

Father Garin received his obedience on October 10, 1862, and arrived in Buffalo on November 26. He met with Bishop Timon. The prelate briefed Father Garin on the difficulties that had occurred, and then his demeanor became very genial. It was now up to the Oblate to tell the bishop how deeply he deplored the recent events, and at the same time, he hoped that intelligent communication would still be possible.[17]

In contrast to the earlier Oblates who had wanted to abandon the work in Buffalo, the new superior judged that it would be awkward to leave after all the sacrifices that had been made to get established there. In his report to Bishop Guigues Father Garin encouraged the provincial to write to France for two more missionaries.[18]

Bishop Guigues apparently became more hopeful. He wrote to the superior general in January that Bishop Timon was sincere in his desire to retain the Oblates at Buffalo. The bishop had even turned down a request from the Lazarist Fathers to engage in retreats, even though they were already established in his diocese. He claimed that this was the work of Oblates.[19]

Father Garin also wrote an enthusiastic letter to the general, noting that their residence occupied the most beautiful site in the city, and that they would soon have to enlarge the church building. He ended by stressing the need for English-speaking missionaries.[20]

* * *

Once he helped to restore peace in Buffalo, as he had done in Plattsburgh, Father Garin faced the task of establishing a permanent residence for the Gray Nuns. The Sisters had been there since October 28, 1857, living in a small residence that Father Chevalier had constructed on Oblate property. It was soon deemed advisable that they have a home of their own. The notes of the provincial council of January 14 and 15, 1863, while Father Garin was superior, mention that the bishop of Buffalo wanted the Gray Nuns to become permanently established in his diocese. Since they had come at the invitation of the Oblates, it was thought fitting to give the sisters a plot of land near the church on the opposite side from the rectory. This land, however, would be ceded to them only if the Oblates were allowed to settle in Buffalo permanently, and only if the land would revert to religious purposes should the Sisters leave the city or move to another site.

Bishop Guigues wrote to the general house, in January 1863, that he found this solution reasonable. Since it was common practice in the United States for each parish to assume the support of its nuns, giving them land was a matter of justice. In the eight years that the Sisters had been in Buffalo, not one penny had been returned to the Mother House, which had borne all the expenditures of the first six years.[21]

Father Garin mentioned the subject again in April. He considered it rightful to help the Sisters since this was also a contribution to education and an appropriate way to use some of the money that had been gathered formerly to build a college.[22]

Everyone agreed that the solution seemed equitable. The provincial council confirmed the decision on September 24, 1863, but only with the provision that the Oblates remain in Buffalo. There were still priests who recommended leaving the area.

At the last minute, the Oblates were unable to turn the land over to the sisters because the bishop wanted this property for other purposes. The priests offered the nuns another site which they were unable to accept. The provincial, Father Florent Vandenberghe, kept Bishop Timon informed of the situation. The nuns themselves were actively seeking a more appropriate location.[23] Once again, a solution was found, thanks to Father Garin's astute leadership and incomparable talent as a conciliator.

Meanwhile, as superior of Buffalo, Father Garin dealt with another issue that was less complicated, but no less apostolic: establishing the Oblates in a German-speaking parish. Negotiations were broached in 1853, when the parish was barely five years old.

That year, Father Garin's letter to the superior general gives us the thread. During a canonical visit to the area, Father Joseph Ambroise Vincens met with Bishop Timon and asked if there could be work for a German Oblate who would be part of the Buffalo community. Father Garin suggested asking for the parish at Blackrock. The bishop refused to commit himself on this parish, but suggested that a priest be allowed to come since there would definitely be work for him. That August, Bishop Timon asked Father Garin about the status of "the German question."

This prompted an immediate letter to Bishop Guigues who replied that Father Vincens had begun proceedings with the major superiors. Bishop Timon assured Father Garin on September 30 that the post of Blackrock was now reserved for his Congregation. Mr. Nickolis Sester, a friend of the Oblates and a founder of that parish, was well acquainted with all of its needs and repeatedly said that the Blackrock parish had a most promising future. Father Garin added that, in a residence like his, with only two people, it was morally impossible to observe the Rule properly. However, with the addition of a German priest and a good English preacher for missions, they all could organize a true Community life. By the same token, the increased revenues from extra ministries would help allay current debts.[24]

Bishop Timon still had to wait two months for a reply to his offer. The project was finally accepted by the Oblates. Father Vandenberghe informed Father Tabaret on April 24, 1864, that Father Martens would take over Blackrock in fifteen days.[25] Everything went according to plan. On May 24, Father Garin wrote to Father Tabaret that Father Henri Martens would be hearing confessions the next day. The Blackrock affair was settled.[26]

Undoubtedly, Father Garin deserves the credit for this accomplishment. He knew how to promote decisive arguments and to skillfully enlighten the judgment of those in authority. Unfortunately, he left Buffalo in 1865, without the opportunity to see the fruition of the work he had begun.

Father Garin's stay in Buffalo provided few apparent consolations for himself personally, but it proved to be a boon for the congregation. This skillful superior nursed a dying parish back to health, which in turn gave birth to a new one.

CHAPTER SIX
THE OBLATE FOUNDATIONS IN LOWELL

Father Garin's accomplishments in the Indian missions and in the parishes of Plattsburgh and Buffalo pale in comparison to his subsequent endeavors. The full measure of his capabilities was finally demonstrated in Lowell where he worked from 1868 until his death.

As a member of the Oblate community in Montreal, Father Garin had been at times assigned to a preaching foray in the United States, accompanied by Father Basile-Jean Dedebant. The "Codex Historicus" of the residence contains the following entry for October 12, 1866: "The Reverend Fathers Garin and Dedebant left for the Boston diocese; during a five to six week period, the two Fathers worked tirelessly among the immigrant French-Canadian population in that part of the United States. They agreed that the spiritual benefits they gained far outweighed their exhaustion.

"The Canadians living in the Massachusetts cities of Springfield, Chicopee, North Adams, South Adams, and Holyoke will never forget the two zealous missionaries. These devout people would have been inconsolable over the departure of priests who did so much good, were it not for the hope of seeing them again."[1]

The general council of the Oblates recorded, on December 12, 1867, that Bishop John Williams of Boston would like to have the Oblates come to his diocese. He wanted to give them a foothold for the preaching of parish missions.

History now provides us with a few glimpses of the events that led Bishop Williams to this decision. At the beginning of that year, there had been some question of establishing a French parish in Lowell for the approximately 1,000 people who had migrated from Canada. They were then being served by St. Patrick's Church. As their numbers increased, the Canadians desired a church where they could hear the Gospel preached in their mother tongue, and where they could feel at home.

While on a business trip to Montreal, Mr. Jean-Baptiste Dozois, carrying a letter of introduction from Bishop Williams, approached Bishop Bourget with this project. Bishop Williams, for his part, had received a delegation of local French immigrants and promised to consider their request. Within a few weeks Father Boissonneau, a diocesan priest from Canada, preached a mission to the Lowell Canadians in the basement of St. Patrick's Church. This was the first attempt to have distinct religious services for the French population.

By an act of Providence, the provincial of the Oblates, Father Florent Vandenberghe, met Bishop Williams on December 8 at the consecration of the cathedral in Burlington, Vermont. The bishop reminded him of the fine work accomplished by Oblate fathers in Boston the previous year, and offered him an establishment in his diocese.

The provincial wasted no time in writing to the general house on December 13: "Bishop Williams of Boston remembers the salutary effects that followed upon the preaching of our priests last year. He would like to receive the Oblates permanently in his diocese. Here is the proposal. He would give us a French parish in an industrial city of forty thousand souls, where there is a large accumulation of Canadians. There are two locations close to Boston in nearly identical circumstances, each having a church that can seat about 900 to 1000 people. I asked his Excellency if our activities would be limited to one parish. He replied that the parish would be mainly a source of steady revenue and that we would be in charge of preaching missions. I then said that you would probably favor such an establishment, since it is our earnest desire to reach out into the States, where religious growth would require and generate an increase of collaborators. I understood that His Excellency would soon be writing to me concerning this matter. To comply, two priests would be needed immediately, and four later. Therefore, without any further delay, Very Reverend Father, I ask that you consider this offer, should you judge the conditions acceptable. It would be relatively easy for us, within a few months, to release two priests for this work. I believe that all the members of our council would be in favor of such an establishment."[2]

The general council began to study this question on December 27 and three days later, Father Pierre Aubert, assistant general, answered in Father Fabre's name. The general council approved this new foundation in principle, but with the proviso that they would examine the conditions at a later time. That is how the provincial received authorization to handle this project with his own council. It was now incumbent upon them to satisfy the general administration with the details and documents needed to make a decision. An agreement was reached that the province alone would assume the burden of this foundation because, for the time being, the general house could not promise financial assistance. However, the province could count on receiving an increase of manpower later in the year, due to the prevailing situation in France. Missionaries there began to lack work and it was feared that this predicament would continue.[3]

The Canadian provincial had written previously to Father Aubert that the foundation in the Boston diocese would be an important and advantageous enterprise. His advisers, Fathers H. Tabaret, J. Antoine and F. Durocher, unanimously favored this establishment. Yet, the details of Bishop Williams' proposals were yet to be heard.[4]

The pace of events quickened. On January 9, 1868, the bishop of Boston informed the provincial that he had started negotiations for the purchase of a church for the Canadians in Lowell and that the transaction might be settled in a few days. "If the negotiations should prove successful, how soon could you send two priests for this church? If you promise the priests, I will send you a note as soon as the transactions are completed. You could then come yourself or send someone else to make the necessary arrangements before the priests' arrival."[5]

Without losing a moment, the provincial wrote to Bishop Williams on January 14. He assured him that everything possible would be done "for the success of this undertaking, which we know to be worthwhile and necessary." Although a community could not be established until the end of the summer, he believed that two priests could be assigned there immediately.[6]

Decidedly, here was a bishop who knew what he wanted and where he was going. The Oblates boldly began stepping up the procedure. In France, on January 20, the superior general declared that Bishop Williams' proposals were most satisfactory.[7] While on January 21 in Montreal, the Provincial had clearly stated his position and that of his council, who were in unanimous agreement. Oblivious for a moment of the ongoing momentous accomplishments of the Oblates in Canada, the provincial went so far as to say: "If we believe the Boston foundation to be worthwhile and timely, it is not because we have many workers, but because we believe that the future development of the Congregation is linked to the United States."[8]

After officially sanctioning a foundation in the Boston diocese, the provincial council sent a copy of the document to the bishop on January 27. He responded simply by calling the provincial to Boston.[9] They agreed during this meeting that a priest would preach a mission in Lowell after Easter, and would spend a few weeks there to study the area's potential. The provincial learned that of the 40,000 to 50,000 inhabitants in Lowell 16,000 were Catholics of whom 3,000 were French Canadians. There are two churches to serve the Irish Catholics in the city: St. Patrick's and St. Peter's. An earlier church, St. Mary's, was now abandoned. The Franco-Americans were offered the choice of buying either St. Mary's or St. Peter's.

Father Vandenberghe found the bishop of Boston to be frank, precise, and straightforward, but his initial plans appeared restrictive. He wanted the priests to deal only with the French Canadians, without ever ministering in

English. The provincial could not agree. To subsist, a community of four religious would require more diversity in its outreach. The Oblates should be permitted to carry on an English-language ministry in the area, if not in the French parish. Otherwise, the priests would become total strangers in a diocese numbering 350,000 Catholics.

Bishop Williams brought Father Garin to Lowell for a tour of the city. They stayed for two days with Father John O'Brien, a saintly man, pastor of St. Patrick's Church. Their private conversations must have been very productive since the bishop now became more flexible and conciliatory. He revised his plan little by little, until it became an entirely new project. The Oblates would now take care of all the Canadians in the city, and one of them would serve in St. John's Hospital as chaplain for three or four years. After that time, the hospital chapel would become an English-only parish for that part of the city, under Oblate care. The priests would henceforth be free to preach missions everywhere in either language. For their part, the Canadians could purchase a Protestant church that was ideally situated in the center of the city. All of this was by way of suggestion, it was up to the Provincial to make the final decisions.

Father Vandenberghe, after much reflection and serious consideration, sent a report to the authorities. The letter went to Father Aubert and concluded: "The situation seems favorable to me. I like the bishop. He appears to deal honestly and without ulterior motives. He does not want to see what some people might call an "unattached church" established in Lowell. I deem the city well located for travel in all directions. Five railways pass through, there are ten daily trips to Boston, and direct service is available to New York and Montreal. I left Montreal at 3:30 in the evening and at 7 o'clock the next morning I was in Lowell... Saint Joseph is the protector of this new mission and I have full confidence in him."[10]

This auspicious beginning pointed toward a satisfactory outcome for all parties concerned. As agreed, two missionaries, Fathers Lucien Lagier and Andre Garin preached a mission in Lowell at the beginning of April.[11]

The opening of that mission was misleading, if we are to believe Father Lagier. Fewer than 640 persons received Communion after eight days of the mission. The adult population seemed to be smaller than at first believed. Although the evening services were well attended, few went to confession. What would the second week be like?

Regardless, the Protestant church was purchased for $11,500. The fund raising was begun, and nearly $2,000 was collected. Father Lagier feared that this was as far as they could go. The people were poor. The missionary began to think they had been too hasty in buying the church. In all probability the Oblates would depart after offering only one Mass there. On the following day they planned to leave for Boston and recommend that a priest from Canada be sought for the poverty-stricken French Catholics of Lowell. Father Lagier did not believe that the Oblates could establish a community there. One diocesan priest would be sufficient. Through it all, the parish priest, Father John O'Brien, had been an excellent host for the Oblates.[12]

This first report was hardly optimistic. Fortunately, the situation improved during the second week and Father Lagier's final evaluation became more enthusiastic. By April 30, he was now looking forward to preaching retreats in Lawrence, East Cambridge, and perhaps elsewhere. He wrote that initially, Father Garin was against the foundation in Lowell. But following an extensive examination of the area, and lengthy reflections on present and future possibilities, Father Garin was leaning more towards the positive side. He would even be willing to lead the undertaking, provided he were given the assistance of a few good men. Once they were installed and better known, the Oblates could radiate throughout the region. Several people advised him to accept, even though conditions did not seem too bright at the beginning. Lowell was a city with a future where there would always be a large French community, especially when the Canadians learned that French-speaking priests would be there.

In all likelihood a beautiful parish could flourish in the environs of St. John's Hospital. Three or four priests would have ample work at the present in Lowell, and in a few years, the Oblate Congregation would have a viable establishment, perhaps even a thriving one. Finally, Father Lagier advised the Provincial that if he decided to establish a foundation in Lowell, he should send a priest as soon as possible to take care of the nascent parish.[13] When Father Garin returned from preaching a short mission in Haverhill, on May 29, he found a letter from the provincial which he answered "that very minute." He was surprised that the provincial never mentioned Father Lagier, since the latter had left on May 11 to report in person to the provincial council with all the facts about Lowell. Father Garin had expected a definitive reply three of four days after the council meeting. It was now going onto three weeks and no news was forthcoming.

He expressed himself simply and frankly. Without judging, he assumed that the provincial had good reasons for his behavior. He had told Father Lagier repeatedly that he would accept the foundation without a moment's hesitation if the decision were favorable.

Father Garin answered the provincial's letter point by point. As for the finances, he believed that the Oblates could count on the generosity of the population. Within three weeks, the Canadians had donated $3,500 toward the purchase of their church. When he dined with Bishop Williams on the occasion of Confirmations during the preceding week, the bishop asked if he had received news from the provincial. Father Garin had answered in the negative while assuring him that he had sent a favorable report and that acceptance by the Oblates was nearly a certainty. "The Bishop seemed pleased," wrote Father Garin, adding his conviction that although Bishop Williams truly wanted the Oblates, he was typically "unemotional" about it as Americans tend to be.

Father Garin continued to extol this project. If the fathers came, they would find more work in Lowell than they could handle. Besides serving two churches and preaching missions in this and neighboring dioceses, they could regularly visit the Canadians in Lawrence, Nashua, Manchester, and Haverhill, as well as other areas. They would visit some of these places on a monthly basis, others every three or four months. An immense area was opening up to their zeal. He then went into details about his recent mission in Haverhill, which lasted four evenings. Communion was given to 182 persons, mostly young shoe-shop workers. These young people were delighted with him, as he with them. The consolation he felt from this was seldom exceeded in his lifetime. He lifted from excommunication twelve couples who had married outside the Church, baptized three adult Americans, one man and two women, as well as seven infants. He also committed himself to a preaching engagement in the Portland diocese.

Bishop Williams finally indicated that he was waiting only for the Oblates' acceptance of the hospital chapel before dividing the city into three parishes. A collection organized by Canadian women yielded $206.00 for the purchase of altar linen, an Irish Catholic donated a chalice, and Father Garin took up a collection on Pentecost Sunday to buy furniture for the rectory.[14]

Father Garin, who would be the master craftsman of this pastoral venture in Lowell, could not have been more enthusiastic. His conviction carried the day. He had every reason to be proud of his first apostolic efforts, yet he tended to downplay his prime role in these early successes. Fortunately, Mr. P. J. Lynch, historian of St. Joseph's Parish provides us with additional details in a book edited by James S. Sullivan.

Mr. Lynch wrote that the driving force behind the outstanding success of this enterprise was indeed the faithful priest, "le Bon Pere" idol of the flock. He is the one to whom Lowell's French colony could justly attribute its emergence as a religious entity.[15] The author then reveals many details which previously had not been acknowledged. There were then about 1,200 Canadians worshiping at St. Patrick's Church. At the start of the mission, on Sunday, April 19, the people were asked if they wanted their own house of worship. Pursuant to their affirmative and enthusiastic response, they were asked if they preferred St. Mary's Church, which was free at that time, or a building on Lee Street owned by the Unitarians. It had been used for religious purposes by the spiritualists, but was now available. The building could be bought at a good price and it was well suited for worship. The Canadians were unanimously in favor of the building on Lee Street, with its brick walls and stone facade.

The next day, Father Garin, accompanied by Joseph Miller and Louis Bergeron, visited a Mr. Bradt who was the administrator for the abandoned church. This gentleman deferred his decision until other committee members could be consulted. Father Garin returned two days later and pushed through a deal at that meeting.[16] The Catholics would pay $11,500, of which $3,000 would be paid upon transfer of the title, and $500 six months later. The balance would be spread out over a period of five years. The Canadians were elated. Father Garin explained the arrangement at the next gathering during the retreat, and announced that money was now needed to complete the negotiations. The response was exuberant and people pledged a substantial amount on the spot. Father Garin paid the $3,000 and completed the transfer of property title by the middle of the week.[17]

Father Garin himself later went over the details of these negotiations. He shared the initial agreements and the signing of the contract with the people "We began a short mission in the basement of St. Patrick's Church. Each evening after the service our good Canadians brought their offerings. Each time I collected $300, $400, even $500, and in the evening I was in the habit of counting the receipts.

"The kindly Father O'Brien always watched me at my task. He would say to me, 'Dear Father Garin, I believe that you count the same $300 each evening.'"

"'No, no, Father,' I replied. 'and I will prove it to you by tallying the $2,000 that I have right here in this bag.'

"'Then, Father Garin, you certainly will succeed in your undertakings, because I confess that my own people could never do as well.'

"Ah, the devotion of my Canadians! They were working for the glory of God! We bought the two little houses next to the church and some time later, a suitable church capable of seating 500 to 600 persons. On Sunday morning we sang the first Mass for Lowell's French Canadians. Father

Lagier officiated, and I played the organ. Many tears flowed that day as the Canadians told one another, 'We are home. We have our own church.'"[18]

Expeditious man that he was, Father Garin had lost no time in completing the transaction.[19] The building was transferred to the new owners on Saturday and everything was prepared for Mass on the next day. On Sunday, May 3, 1868, the pulpit from the old church was turned towards the back wall to serve as a temporary altar. A communion rail was improvised. Everything was ready so that a joyous and grateful people could kneel at Mass in a church that was truly theirs. Father Garin wasn't feeling well that morning, so Father Lagier presided at the altar. Since it was the feast of the Solemnity of Saint Joseph, the great saint was declared patron of the new church. Father Vandenberghe's confidence in Saint Joseph had been well placed; with this saint's patronage any task is possible.

At a later time, remembering these events and the joy of the Canadians, Father Garin remarked to Mr. Lynch that one could easily imagine we were worshiping in one of the old parishes of Canada."[20] Directly after Mass, Father Garin collected pew rents for the 500 seats in the church.

These accomplishments, at the end of April and the beginning of May, were so remarkable that we can readily understand the enthusiasm conveyed in the letter of May 29, which we have been quoting.

Believing that he had not been explicit enough in his first letter to the provincial, Father Garin wrote again on the next day, May 30, 1868, to provide more details. He explained that he had just returned from preaching and was tired from lack of sleep. For the past three or four days he had been hearing confessions late into the night, then rising for an early Mass in the morning.

He stated that after a good night's sleep, he was in "tip-top," shape as they say in Lowell. Father Garin was already picking up local expressions as he began to feel at home in this country. He added that the Oblates had nothing to fear from establishing themselves here. The area was opening up before them as an immense field for an exceptional harvest of souls, and a truly miraculous catch. The Canadians who had settled throughout the wider region, numbering several hundred thousands, were calling upon the Oblates from all sides. How could the provincial refuse? After all, what is the purpose of an Oblate house if not "the salvation of the most abandoned souls, the glory of God, the extension of Catholicism, and the welfare of our Congregation"? He concludes: "These should be our motives, I assume, and we have all of them right here."

"What makes me consider Lowell an especially good establishment is that an Irish parish will also be entrusted to us. We will have a solid basis of operation. Father Lagier must have mentioned to you that the Augustinians are building a magnificent church in Lawrence. It will leave them indebted for more than $150,000. They do not seem the least bit worried about the success of their undertaking. They have been in the country for a long time and in addition to this parish, they have only a small chapel a few miles from Lawrence. They have no revenue from missions and retreats as we do.

"You tell me that the great problem is the shortage of workers. I have nothing to say since I am not aware of your personnel resources, but since you proposed a community to the bishop and not simply a pastor, you must have had a few individuals in mind whom you hoped to send. You asked me how long I could function here with just one other priest. I cannot give you a definite answer. You know of my aversion to small two-member communities. But in the final analysis, if we had to spend a month or two, or even a little longer in that precarious state, we could find the patience, providing we had the hope or promise of one or two good individuals to come.

"Since Father Lagier is a member of the provincial council, he informed me that I could have Father Debruel if I wanted. However, I think that this could not happen until after the school year. I believe he would do well here. He is very fluent in both languages, a good preacher, good musician, has a gracious demeanor, etc. etc. I think he might enjoy it here.

"I would willingly accept an assignment here because I consider it promising and beneficial to the Church and to the Congregation. But I have no desire to be weighted down with individuals who would not work in union with me. You know the kind of men that are required for this country...

"The bishop has told me officially that our acceptance was the only delay before dividing the city into parishes. The three or four years during which we serve the Sisters of St. John's Hospital in their chapel will give us the time to plan the construction of our parish church. Please forward a decision as soon as possible, because I am holding up my attempts to rent a house and furnish it. My plan includes having the Canadians from our outreaches in Nashua, Manchester, etc., contribute towards the Lowell foundation if it were to take place, but I cannot proceed since I have nothing official."[21]

It would be difficult to find a person with more enthusiasm, resoluteness, and holiness. He gained the support of the provincial who had seemed seriously hesitant, judging by the questions he asked in his letter of May 24th. By June 10th, Father Vandenberghe felt obliged to take action. He wrote to

41

Father Aubert, "It becomes urgent for us to commit ourselves to refuse or accept the Lowell mission. The more we analyze the situation, the more we foresee the benefits of venturing into this country. But what can we do, with so few men to fall back on? Please help us and we shall be a source of honor for the congregation."[22]

The provincial may have been wary for awhile, but before long all hesitation disappeared. He informed Bishop Williams on June 18 that the province accepted the missions in the area and the two undertakings in Lowell.[23] The next day he wrote to the superior general, Father Fabre, "The Lowell establishment is moving ahead. There is no formal contract yet with the bishop of Boston and I doubt that he wants one. He will put us in charge of the work to be done, and will do so with generosity. The bishop still needs to have certain administrative concerns cleared up, but I am convinced that he wants us as a community and that he will help us.[24] Although we may be short of personnel at the moment, our priests have all agreed to move ahead this year, in view of the tremendous good that can be done. Father Garin will be revitalized; I am sending him Father Guillard as a partner. This arrangement will allow three priests in residence for community life, though two of them may be busy at parish missions."[25]

The Oblates were officially established in the Diocese of Boston on June 26, 1868.[26] A few days later, on June 30, Father Garin briefed the provincial on the arrangements with Bishop Williams. Before going into the details, he mentioned how his new companion was overwhelmed by the beauty of the Lowell surroundings. He added that the Oblates were staying in the Sisters' residence as of the preceding Saturday. Their two rooms would be fine until they had their own home.

Bishop Williams counted on Father Garin to communicate with the provincial. Father Vandenberghe wanted to know under what conditions the Oblates were accepted in the diocese. Father Garin to informed the provincial "that he entrusted us with ministry to the Canadians and the service of St. John's Hospital chapel, which, as of last Sunday, enjoys all the privileges of a parish church. He told me that he would come to Lowell on July 6 and that if Father John O'Brien and Father Goudden were in agreement, (he was sure that they would be) he would divide the city into parishes. Should some objection arise, we would be equal parties to the discussion and could claim all that is rightfully ours. I believe it is the wish of these pastors that the city be so divided, at least as far as Rev. O'Brien is concerned. He mentioned this to me when I informed him of my visit to Boston. The bishop again spoke to me of BellaRica (Sic) the small mission I mentioned earlier, which is four or five miles from Lowell. There is no hurry on this though, since nothing has been done yet towards the chapel. When the time comes, I will let you know, so we can have Father McGrath come to give a short retreat. He could also preach in Lowell, at our St. John's Chapel. This would be one way of making him known in Massachusetts."[27]

Father Garin ended his letter saying that the celebration of the Saint Jean-Baptiste festival this year had been a tremendous success, "without hard liquor" and without quarrels. The people said that there had never been an evening like it in Lowell where so much decorum and orderliness were observed.

The provincial did not answer until July 13. He willingly empowered the Oblates to follow the bishop's wishes concerning the third parish to be created and entrusted to the Oblates. He enjoined Father Garin to do his utmost for the success of this important work. However, until the bishop issued the official documents accepting the Oblates as a Community with regular canonical rights and privileges, the provincial could only consider the task of the Oblates in Lowell as a temporary mission. It could be suspended at will. He advised Father Garin not to interrupt his work even though a formal community could not be established in Lowell until the canonical rights and privileges had been guaranteed. There was reasonable hope that the protocols would soon be observed.[28]

The bishop did not wait for these formalities to set the Oblates to work. The Episcopal Register 1856-1888 records that on July 5, 1868, the Oblates served at St. John's Chapel, St. Joseph's Church, and the mission of North Billerica.[29]

A new House was henceforth founded in Lowell, although the canonical recognition by the provincial was issued only later on November 1, 1868,[30] and by Bishop Williams, on June 19, 1869.[31] The enterprise was a resounding success: audacious but prudent, slow but progressive. The credit must be attributed almost entirely to Father Garin's talent, tenacity, and spiritual dynamism.

The history of this foundation would be incomplete without recognizing another agent, whose impact was truly providential: Father Leclerc. He was a diocesan priest and a seminary confrere of Boston's bishop. The friends met in Burlington, Vermont, at the consecration of the new cathedral. The bishop told Father Leclerc that many French Canadians lived in his diocese. He believed that there were enough of them in Lowell to form a separate parish. He ended by asking for help in finding a French-Canadian priest for them. "Wouldn't it be a good idea," replied his friend, "to ask the Oblates in

Montreal? They are trained for this particular kind of work. I will introduce you to their provincial, Father Vandenberghe. He is here now. You could discuss this with him."[32]

Providence must have wanted this timely referral, as it led to the marvelous results that are known to us today. Lowell became, for the Oblates a center of substantial influence, a nursery for vocations and an entirely new religious province, the first in the United States.

CHAPTER SEVEN
FROM TEMPORARY STATE TO PERMANENT STATUS

The Lowell undertaking seemed to be off to a good start, but it lacked an official basis for permanency. No agreement had been signed between Boston and Montreal. Mutual admiration and confidence were in the air, but not without a certain amount of gray area, and latent insecurity. One wonders how the work could continue and even advance. The existing records and the constant activity lead us to conclude that everything revolved around a man seemingly at rest, but exuding a quiet and serene energy that was sure of itself. The mainspring of the Oblate foundation in Lowell was certainly Father Andre Garin, OMI. His leadership left everything clear, simple and in its place. He wielded an astonishing magnetism when dealing with superiors, colleagues and subordinates that somehow charmed them into thinking as he thought, and needing what he needed. We shall observe how he evolved during this critical year in which his patience and energy were severely tested, but where his determination and native common sense once again prevailed.

On July 15, Father Garin wrote to Montreal, "Since Father Cosson's arrival, we have been living in two pleasant rooms at the hospital, which is also the home of the Daughters of Charity. I am thinking of renting a house that would suit us well. Only the width of the street would separate us from the Sisters' chapel. Even though the weather is sweltering and we are alone in serving our respective churches, we are in reasonably good health and we shall get by. Father Cosson has already conducted two services in his Irish chapel and has preached on those two occasions. They understand and like him. He is happy here."

Father Garin then insisted on reinforcement, in view of Bishop Williams' offer of the Billerica mission. He did not expect the income from the English-speaking parishes to increase that first year. People would most likely continue to have their children baptized at the other churches until parish lines were clearly drawn. Secondly, the expenses of three priests would increase very little over those of two. The rent would be the same ($250 per year), as well as the cost of heating, the salaries of the hired help, and so on. He concluded his letter by noting that the local pastors had not responded to the bishop regarding the division of parishes; upon their approval, he intended to give the Oblates a parish with specific boundaries. Father Garin planned to ask for an even wider area since there were few Irish parishioners in the Belvidere and Centralville sections of the city.[1]

In spite of his warmth and good will, Bishop Williams seemed obstinate in not writing to the provincial. He preferred to negotiate in person with Father Garin, who then faithfully transmitted the details to Father Vandenberghe.

All during this time effective work was going on in Lowell, and everything ran smoothly in that "dear house," as Father Fabre called it.[2] On August 3, Father Garin announced that he would go to Boston the following week to clarify the parish boundaries. He had a census taken of the Belvidere and Centralville sections of the city after the bishop offered to cede these as an Oblate parish for the English speaking. The Irish in these areas numbered less than 300 families, a very small portion of all the Catholics in Lowell. He therefore proposed that the new boundaries include all of Sections No. 2 and No. 6 of the city. Belvidere was all of No. 6, but Centralville was only a portion of No. 2. By expanding the borders to all of No. 2, 300 more families would be added. The French church would now be included in the expanded territory.[3]

Father Garin wrote to the provincial two weeks later to reassure him about the bishop. "I do not believe that the bishop of Boston is against us or that he plans to interpret the canonical laws exclusively to his advantage. It seems to me that he merely wants to avoid the ordeal of dictating conditions such as those you mentioned in your letter to him. He purely and simply wants us in his diocese. At the first opportunity, I shall try to learn if the other communities have made similar agreements with the diocesan authorities."[4] In closing, Father Garin asked for a third priest to fulfill the anticipated requests for missions. He suggested the name of Father Jean Marc Guillard, who subsequently joined them at the beginning of winter.

The division of the parishes took a long time, but that did not deter the priests from pursuing their tasks among the Irish, and even with encouraging results. The hospital chapel soon proved to be too small. The only alternatives were expansion or a new construction. The nuns owned the chapel, and the major problem was to determine who would assume responsibility for the expansion.

Father Garin stated his case to the provincial on October 8. He believed that the time had come to enlarge the sisters' chapel. Sister Rose, the local superior, went to Boston to confer with the bishop. He refused to commit himself and asked to see Father Garin. In the course of their meeting the bishop indicated that he had refused to give the nuns permission to expand the building, until they reached an agreement with the Oblates. This would preclude future problems or misunderstandings. The bishop preferred to leave matters as they were, namely, that the Oblates would defray the costs of expansion through contributions from their own Congregation. This would leave room for future projects with local funds.

The local sister superior and Father Garin talked the matter over. It was decided that she would write to her own superiors to submit this project.[5]

On October 10, the Oblate provincial answered simply that it was up to the sisters to assume responsibility for the undertaking.[6] Fortunately, on the following day, he had enough sense to consult Father Aubert, the assistant general in France. He wrote, "Another matter must be dealt with in Lowell. The bishop intends to divide the city into parishes, which would be to our advantage. But now the provisional chapel of St. John's, which belongs to the Sisters of the hospital, is inadequate. It was suggested that the building be enlarged at our expense."[7]

The general administration reacted with magnanimity. Father Aubert answered that they had already decided to make the establishment in Lowell as secure as possible. To this end, the provincial was entirely free to choose the most effective means to consolidate the task and make it thrive.[8] Father Fabre, for his part, on November 9, bestowed on Father Vandenberghe the authorization to erect the residence of the Oblates as a canonical house whenever he judged the moment opportune.[9]

Even before receiving a response from Paris, Father Vandenberghe went to Boston for an interview with Bishop Williams. He later recorded the results of that interview. The Oblates were accepted into the diocese as missionaries. They were authorized to preach in French and in English, even though the principal reason for the Lowell foundation was the large number of French Canadians living in the area. The bishop entrusted St. Joseph's and St. John's Churches, as well as the temporary service of North Billerica, to the superior of the Lowell community, who would henceforth be looked upon as the representative of the Congregation. The superior could see to these tasks himself, or through the members of his community.[10]

Nothing more could be asked for, short of an official document in writing. The provincial accepted the bishop at his word and everything was finalized. He established a formal community on November 1, appointing Father Garin as the first superior of the Lowell Oblates.

Father Vandenberghe lost no time in relaying his impressions to the superior general: "God be praised! I have just celebrated the twentieth anniversary of my religious vows by founding a new community. I am sure you will approve of our decisions. Our province will now have an additional establishment, rich in hope and already very productive...I have been in Lowell for eight days. The bishop of Boston was away, and I was not able to meet him until last Friday. I can only praise His Excellency's kindness and thoughtfulness. He seems to reach out to us with full and complete trust. His benevolence is not simply a matter of words. When I asked him for official letters of institution, he told me to prepare them myself and he would gladly sign them.

"As for the community of Fathers Garin, Guillard, Lebret and Cosson, it seemed urgent to me to set it up without delay."[11]

The provincial continued his letter with an overview of the population of Lowell. He speaks of its religious structure, and then describes its two Oblate churches: St. Joseph's, seating 600, and St. John's, 400. When the bishop granted the French church to the Oblates as a parish, he also elevated St. John's chapel to a parish church. The provincial hoped that St. John's would serve 700 to 800 English speaking families, or at least 500 to 600, depending on the new parish boundaries. On the other hand St. Joseph's Church would serve all the French Canadians of the city.

The provincial's visit to Lowell was primarily motivated by his concern for St. John's Chapel. He ended by agreeing with Father Garin's view, that the Oblates should be responsible for additions to the chapel, while paying rent to the sisters for its use. The details of this master plan were yet to be worked out with the nuns, as the day to day relationships remained most cordial. He added, "My greatest consolation was to see the devotion of the people. I was deeply moved on those two Sundays when I was able to observe them. Both of our churches proved to be too narrow at all the services. This morning there were three to four hundred Communions at the French church. The Irish are equally enthusiastic and love their new church. It would take a long Chapter indeed to describe the good that our Congregation can and will accomplish here, under the protection of the Blessed Virgin." He closed with these words: "I ask you, Very Reverend Father, to endorse and bless our new foundation. Father Garin will write to you himself. He will describe to you more aptly than I can what a great city Lowell is, and what great deeds we are accomplishing there."[12]

In early 1869, the provincial council decided that it was time to start building in Lowell. But nothing could be done in view of the ongoing negotiations between the nuns and Father Garin about finances. The priest's tact, however, was on the verge of surmounting all obstacles. On January 11, he was able to reassure the provincial. Bishop Williams believed the offer made to the nuns was fair and liberal, and he was of the opinion that the local sister superior would accept.[13] In fact, both parties finally signed the hoped for agreement on January 22. The priests would utilize the chapel for a four-year period, starting April 1, 1869, after which time a parish church must be available elsewhere.[14]

A major point was scored and it was a very important step forward. Father Garin hastened to notify the provincial: "The axe is now at the foot of the tree. This very week I expect to contract for the expansion of the chapel." With this new arrangement the chapel will seat 900, by moving the sacristy back into a 20 foot extension which covers the full width of the building. The total cost will be $2,000 to $2,500. This construction will be completed around March 20. Along with this, Father Garin busied himself with what he called "la question delicate" and "la grande question": finding acreage for a future church. There were in fact no totally suitable sites to be found.[15]

Father Garin ended his letter with a request for a fourth priest, reminding the provincial that preaching missions was the first purpose of the Lowell foundation.[16] He was on target, because at the clergy retreat, Bishop Williams recommended to his priests that they entrust their parish retreats to the Oblate Fathers.

Very little is known about the months that followed. The official archives remain silent. But we do chance upon a letter, dated June 20, the day after Bishop Williams canonically instituted the Oblate community into the diocese.[17] It was a communication from the provincial to the general house: "I have been in Lowell for three days...Yesterday, I went to see the bishop of Boston who showed himself more and more pleased and benevolent. I don't know how, but our missionaries are stirring up quite a commotion in these parts; some say that they are sowing discord. As you know, the most noticeable failing in the ranks of the clergy is not only the presence of unworthy priests. Lack of zeal is perhaps the greatest drawback to the practice of religion. Our parish missions are such an unusual experience that everyone is shaken up. I believe that the bishop understands this very well and is pleased with the results. He is by temperament a frank person, and seldom speaks. Each word therefore becomes precious and effective. I was very impressed with the reception the bishop gave us, and he, in turn, shared with us how pleased he was with our priests. I handed him the agreement, a copy of which I am sending to you. He read and signed it saying: 'This is exactly what I had been thinking.'"

"We shall now have to consider buying a plot of land on which to build a church, and thus establish a firm base. Fathers McGrath and Mangin preached a mission to the Irish in our chapel, and distributed Communion to 6,000 people. They could have doubled this number if more priests had been available."[18]

It is truly remarkable how many enterprises were undertaken and how many obstacles surmounted in the narrow space of one year. Once again, we are forced to conclude that Father Garin made known all the resources of his rare intelligence and compassionate heart.

Archbishop John Williams of Boston

Former St. Jean Baptiste Rectory

CHAPTER EIGHT
IMMACULATE CONCEPTION CHURCH

With the construction of a church in mind, Father Garin lunged into the search for available land. Nothing could stop him. We get the picture from the letters that flowed between Lowell, Montreal and Paris during the summer of 1869. On July 1, he shared with his provincial how he had obtained a plot of land that was familiar to them both. Three weeks later, he wrote that he almost acquired a large tract of land at the foot of the hill, but the owners, the Massachusetts Mills Company, had second thoughts and refused to sell. Other plans began to brew. In August, he rejoiced over the purchase of a new lot, along with serious prospects for procuring neighboring houses and adjacent plots.[1] His laconic manner of describing the area leads us to suspect that the two men often paced the environs together and had made their own survey.

Two months later, the provincial sent a summary of Father Garin's purchases to the superior general. It was at the moment an impressive tract of land with nearly 300 feet of frontage. With a little more negotiating, the plot could become a perfect quadrangle, sufficiently large for a church and a residence.[2] By early November, Father Garin ended up with 326 feet of frontage, with a maximum depth of 120 feet. The land included two vacant lots and a few buildings: one three-decker house, two double-deckers, and a cottage.

Writing to the superior general, the provincial extolled the remarkable talents of the new superior in Lowell. This man "had contrived with uncanny skill" to circumvent stumbling blocks of every kind. At times Father Garin was obliged to detour into as many as six transactions for one single purchase. This was necessary in order to thwart certain greedy neighbors who would certainly have doubled their price had they known of a project to consolidate these properties. In less than four months the superior was not only positioned to build a church, but he was able to do so in the most desirable location possible, right in the midst of the parishioners.

The members of his religious community were adequately housed, even if only for a time, in two flats of the three-story building. The rooms and living space were decent. They set up a chapel where they could now recite the Divine Office daily.[3] The one admonition the provincial had for the thriving Oblate community in Lowell was that for some months they had neglected to preach parish retreats.[4] That negligence could not be attributed to Father Garin who was already doing the work of four.

Even though the provincial could mention his complaint, Bishop Williams was roundly pleased. The bishop seemed convinced that with a leader like Father Garin, the Oblates could only be successful in whatever they undertook. In order to help defray the cost of these early purchases and allow the parish to forge ahead with the construction of a church, the bishop suggested an immediate appeal to the people. Businesses were thriving in Lowell; seize the opportunity! Why not a gigantic bazaar?

The provincial did not agree. It seemed to him that to begin by collecting funds was putting the plow before the oxen. The bishop had first to decide how he would divide the city into parishes, and what kind of parish he would give the Oblates. Only then could they begin to envision a church suited to the needs of the Congregation and determine how to best utilize the land at their disposal.

Another detail wearied the provincial. Until now, the acquisitions had been made on a family basis, whereby the last survivor would inherit everything.[5] This type of ownership could not go on, the Lowell community had to incorporate. In Massachusetts, where the law was more liberal, American citizenship was not required of all the members of a corporation. Hence, incorporation was possible. This was not the case in other states, such as New York.

While waiting for answers to all these questions, Father Garin's clear mind and practical judgment brought everyone to focus on one theme: moving forward. At once the Lowell priests became involved in a subscription campaign. Father Guillard gave it his all, lugging his heavy briefcase from house to house. He was usually well received, but at times was rebuffed and humiliated. Nevertheless, the results were gratifying. If donations continued at the same pace, the foundations of the church could be laid in the Fall.[6] That was their thought on May 31, 1870; but by July, Father Guillard began to hope that they might even be ready that summer. To all appearances this undaunted fund collector was trying to move faster than his leader. The subscription so far was most gratifying. By July, the full amount of $12,000 for the real estate had been paid, more than $20,000 was pledged.[7] Finally, a grand bazaar yielded $6,000 in net proceeds.[8]

Unfortunately, this flow of activity ran into unexpected major snags. Father Garin had decided to utilize the services of P.C. Keely. Despite his renown as an architect, the man had little regard for timetables. This trait led to many complications. First he complained that the site was inadequate for the type of construction he envisioned. This would require the purchase of a few bordering lots. The bishop of Boston came to the aid of the dejected father superior who no longer knew which saint to invoke. Bishop

Williams used his personal influence to persuade a Boston financial company to sell a strip of its property to the Oblates.[9] The transaction, which added just the right amount of land, was completed in February 1871. The work could begin at last. Every effort would now be made to have the church basement available for worship within a year.[10]

The Provincial in Montreal, Father Vandenberghe, sang a different tune. He needed to see the plans. Father Garin could only answer, "I am as troubled as you are by the architect's delays." This gentleman had come to Lowell in August. It was now March of the following year. He did send in a plan for the facade in December, but noted that the property was not wide enough for the transepts. The additional lots could only be purchased by February, therefore, Mr. Keely had only been at work for a few weeks. He was not easy to handle, but his monetary demands were not unreasonable. Father Garin had found it necessary to plead with him to work on this construction. The architect accepted with the understanding that just the basement would be built during the first year. Only the plans for that portion were needed. Father then added that the only precise dimensions he had on hand for the future church were the outside length of 205 feet, the width at the transepts of 100 feet, and the height of the ceiling in the lower church at 15 feet.[11]

The Provincial must have had reservations about these dimensions. On March 24, Father Garin seemed surprised at the problems that were raised. At the council meeting in May 1870, which he attended, the matter of limiting the dimensions to a length of 150 feet was not brought up. The only restriction was that the church would not seat more than 1,800 people. Father Garin could now ask the architect for a Gothic-style church, with transepts, and a seating capacity of 1,800. The architect adjusted the dimensions and based his calculations on these requirements.[12]

In April, Father Garin was finally able to forward a preliminary sketch to give the provincial an idea of the future church, and to ask for his approval or suggestions for appropriate changes. The provincial answered only that he could not decide until he had the opportunity to examine complete and detailed plans.[13] He was less critical on the next day, however, in a letter to Father Fabre, the superior general.[14] He admitted that his attitude towards Father Garin's plans in Lowell was pressured by the number of Oblate churches under construction at the same time in Canada: Notre Dame in Hull, Maniwaki, and Saint Sauveur in Quebec. The Provincial was also seeking funds for the construction of a novitiate. As for Lowell, he had no fears about the financial risks involved, nor did he in the least intend to defeat the project. He was torn in all directions and felt the need to tighten the reins on so many Oblates who wanted to build. Each priest looked only at his own immediate enterprise and was pressing to go on.[15]

The provincial apparently found the existing plans somewhat too grand. Bishop Williams, on the other hand, was very pleased with them.[16] The work was under way by May 18. No time was lost in choosing white granite from Concord, New Hampshire. The foundations were almost finished on the East Merrimack Street side by May 29.[17] The work progressed at a slow pace. The blessing of the corner stone had been planned for August 15, but was postponed to October 15. Father Vandenberghe, accompanied by Bishop Guigues of Ottawa, traveled to Lowell for the ceremony. Unfortunately, the rite had to be canceled for the moment, at the request of the mayor of the city. He entreated the fathers to forego any public gathering because of a smallpox epidemic that was ruthlessly ravaging the city. The superior found consolation, nevertheless, in the thought that Bishop Guigues had been able to see the project and that he was delighted with it.[18]

Father Garin was distressed by the lack of details in the construction plans, but the provincial was even more so. From Paris, Father Pierre Aubert, the assistant general, wanted to see the plans, and ordered that they be forwarded to him. The provincial replied evasively on November 10, that he could do nothing about the situation. He explained that he did not possess a complete set himself. The architect handed them out one section at a time, and up to now had supplied only general data such as the dimensions of the building, its approximate cost, etc. Everyone was proceeding cautiously. The size of the building was reduced from 205 to 184 feet. For the moment, the parish was not a penny in debt and was holding a substantial financial reserve. What could be better? The architect was deserving of their complete trust, even though the possibility of additional expenditures was not excluded.[19]

For whatever reason, conscience maybe, the provincial forwarded what sketches he had on hand to the assistant general a few days later. He asked openly whether or not the work should continue.

While these discussions were going on across the Atlantic, Father Garin moved forward in Lowell. The blessing of the corner stone finally took place on November 30. Bishop Williams presided over the magnificent ceremony. More than 2,000 persons attended even though the temperature hovered between 15 and 20 degrees below zero.[20]

After only one quiet day of rest, the turmoil began anew. Again the beleaguered priest was inconvenienced by his Canadian authorities for detailed plans. For once, he was on the verge of giving up. His letter of December 4, 1871, to the Provincial was that of a man who was annoyed, but much too practical to continue in the face of an insurmountable obstacle.

He wrote, "In this matter, I have done everything I could. I have written to Mr. Keely. I have explained to him in person that I am a religious, that I cannot do things without approval. It is absolutely necessary that the plans be submitted to and approved by my Superiors in Canada and in France. He understands all that. He promises us anything we want, then he keeps none of his promises. We are not the only ones treated thus. He is the same with everyone else; bishops are no different. Then why not hire another architect? Why continue with him? Because there is none other who is a true architect. Murphy of Providence, whom we were on the point of hiring ourselves, recently built a church in Connecticut that collapsed just a few weeks ago. Mr. Keely, despite his delays, is still the best and the only one to employ for the designing of large churches. I have done everything possible to obtain the plans. I am still trying to get them. He has promised, but, to tell the truth, I have no hope of getting them, except piece by piece as needed to build. Such are matters at this moment. If the superior general deems it appropriate to stop the work, we shall not continue a single day beyond his order. Or again, if you think that another priest will have more influence than I do with Keely to obtain the plans, I am ready to yield to him. Do not be afraid to offend me by removing me from here. Certainly, when confronting the common good individual interests must disappear."[21]

This may well have been the most honest and well thought out letter that the provincial ever received. It impressed him so much that he felt sufficiently bolstered to answer Father Aubert's overwhelming letters. Without delay, he took pen in hand and brought out into the open a multitude of considerations. Among the topics, he mentioned that thrift is a guiding principle. The priests were not anticipating a palatial church, but one that is respectable and in conformity with felicitous artistic rules. All were in agreement that expensive sculptures and purely fanciful embellishments must be avoided. "You see", he continued, "the question can be simplified. The architect is truly good, although lazy. He prefers to study each section separately. So far, I have found him to function admirably without running us into needless expenses. Can we continue, leaving him alone and trusting in him? As far as I am concerned, we cannot do otherwise. If he were to give us a complete plan, I doubt that he would follow it. The work is overseen irreproachably. The architect himself awards all the contracts. From this standpoint, our priests face no complications or worries.[22]

That letter clinched everything. Father Aubert finally understood the situation and advised the provincial to go ahead.[23] Father Garin was finally given free rein. The Lowell superior had proved that he could see clearly into problems. He knew what he was doing and was able to grasp what he had to do.

Three months later, in February 1872, the provincial went to Lowell for a lengthy inspection of the work. On his return, he communicated his impressions to the assistant general. The church basement would soon be finished, but because the building materials had to be completely dry, it could not be occupied for a few months. He added: "You see, everything has gone well up to now. All the stones necessary to continue the work have been purchased, delivered, and paid for. We know what the architect has in mind because the dimensions have now been restricted by the size of the lower church. You now know the basic plans: the quality of the stones, the type of masonry...but Keely is not a man to do a day's work ahead of time, he moves when he has to. The cost of the stonework will be approximately $30,000. This figure will remain constant. Of course there are many advantages to having a job done at once rather than in sections, that is what has given rise to our problem." [24]

The letter dared not say so, but it was now clear that Father Garin had been right all along. In the face of obstacles, he did not stop to grope but went right to work. The lower church was opened for worship a few months later, according to plan, on the first Sunday of July, 1872. Bishop Williams presided at the blessing, preached at High Mass and administered Confirmation during the day. The crypt could seat 1,900 persons. The work had cost $45,000.[25]

Once the basement was finished, thoughts were turned immediately to the construction of the upper church. For the next few years, due perhaps to the abating of problems or to the lack of keeping historical records, the exchange of letters diminished. Apprehensions ceased, the major authorities no longer intervened, and the contractors were free to do their work. Bottom line: everything rested on Father Garin's strong shoulders. It finally became apparent that he embodied talent, common sense, kindness, patience, daring, and above all, hard work and tenacity. He found an extraordinary collaborator in Mr. Keely, because he was able to understand that enigmatic architect and to extract the utmost from him.

As the church began to rise its beauty thrilled everyone. A few years along, Father Joseph Mangin happened to mention in a letter: "We are completing one of the most beautiful churches in the country in honor of the Immaculate Conception." The letter is dated November 30, 1876, when the construction was entering into its fifth year. Hopefully, it would be ready for worship by the following Spring.[26] Archbishop Williams had designated early June for the consecration.

As foreseen, the archbishop presided with full solemnity on June 10, 1877, assisted by the bishops of Burlington and Springfield. The Oblate provincial, who was now Father Joseph Antoine, said he was quite proud, and added that it was one of the most beautiful churches in the United States, including the cathedrals. It's amazing how this much beauty can be achieved by respecting the simple laws of style, and without adding fancy trimmings or meaningless baubles.[27]

The story is told that on the same day, an elated Father Garin returned to the church alone. There, in the simplicity of his heart, he offered this humble prayer: "Lord, I have accomplished little in my life, please allow me to offer You at least this monument through the hands of Mary Immaculate."[28]

It was no ordinary monument he was offering to God in honor of Mary Immaculate. An article featured in "Missions des Oblats" for 1877 meticulously describes this remarkable church. After providing the dimensions, with which we are already familiar, the author points out the 16 graceful pillars upholding the vault, the 322 benches each accommodating six people, the floors of Georgia pine, and the lighting provided by 430 gold-plated gas sconces affixed to the pillars. Outside light filters in through colorful stained glass windows, seven of which surround the sanctuary, portraying the Sacred Heart, the Immaculate Conception, Saint Anne, Saint Elizabeth, Saint Joachim, Saint Joseph, and Saint John the Baptist. Along the nave, the windows portray Saint Peter, Saint Paul, Saint Andrew, Saint Patrick, Saint Martin and the beggar, Moses striking the rock, and Jesus in the midst of children.

We interrupt the description here, to say the author of the article neglected to mention that this admirable choice of tableaux revealed Father Garin's most cherished devotions and most sensitive heart. He was remembering his beloved France in the windows of the Sacred Heart and Saint Martin. The former recalled the Montmartre church which his Oblate brothers were erecting in Paris, and the latter was a legendary apostle of France. Peter and Paul evoke the universal Church; Andrew was his patron saint; the Immaculate Conception was his Oblate title. Then one can identify the patron saints of the French Canadians, the Irish, all Christian workers, mothers of families, and charitable works. Moses and the rock expressed his trust in Divine Providence, and finally, Jesus teaching the little children symbolized the schools that the worthy Catholics of Lowell were actually building under their pastor's leadership. But now, back to the article we were consulting.

The Gothic-style altar structure measures 18 feet in width and reaches up 21 feet towards the ceiling. It is one of the most beautiful works of religious art in Massachusetts, combining up to twelve varieties of marble. The tabernacle door is of gilt copper, as are the cross and the large candlesticks. The organ has three keyboards of 58 notes each, a 30-note pedal board, 54 sets, and 45 stops. The total cost of the church was $175,000, not including the towers.

The author of the article provides us with certain other details unavailable elsewhere. On dedication day, 2,500 persons found comfortable seating in the church. Although it was on a Sunday, 24 priests were able to attend. The bishop of Burlington preached a very eloquent sermon praising Mary Immaculate. His many references to the Oblate Missionaries were much more than mere oratory.[29]

There were many written accounts of this celebration but one point interests us: what were the sentiments of Boston's archbishop? As usual, he had little to say, smiling in his quiet dignity. Being an admirer of architectural beauty and successful enterprises, he could but bathe in the pride and joy of the moment. Inwardly, he must have congratulated himself for putting complete trust in Father Garin and his team, for having occasionally lent a deaf ear to the Provincial, and for not cluttering his office with compromising paperwork. Too many written agreements, too many signed guarantees, and too many blue-sky projections can paralyze spontaneous action. He could only be grateful for those decisions taken day by day under his very eyes by his cherished Oblate Fathers of Lowell. Archbishop Williams was certainly pleased. If he ceded the pulpit to the bishop of Burlington, it could be that he feared his heart might break out in tears before the assembly. Everything registered in his steadfast memory. Seven years later, without a moment's hesitation, he entrusted a second English-speaking church to the same Oblates. It was Sacred Heart parish, in the Farm City area of Lowell. This parish was established on January 1, 1884, and was immediately placed in their hands to build and organize. Father Garin was not directly connected with this project, but it came in the wake of his success in 1877 at Immaculate Conception Church.

Father Garin was not overwhelmed by the endless flow of praise that came upon the heels of his accomplishment. Yet, with the great common sense that characterized him, he could say to Father Fabre, the superior general, "I believe it is one of the most beautiful churches entrusted to our Congregation."[30] This magnificent church, which, after a hundred years, is still the pride of the city Lowell, and was duplicated in Hull, Canada, was conceived and brought to life in his mind and heart. The person responsible for such an achievement deserves a place in history.

With this construction and its related problems behind him, Father Garin recalled that during a canonical visit from the general house, Father Soulier had included in his report the need for Catholic schools. The document stated that necessary steps should be taken as soon as possible to provide Catholic schools for Lowell's children. This idea apparently did not spring from a simple impression but resulted from serious study. The visitor had recommended the construction of an unadorned brick building, not to begin before the spring of 1878. The date was now past, it was time to work. The land was purchased by the end of May, but nothing happened for eighteen long months. The problems must have been enormous.

This time, Father Garin was immersed in a domain where the balance of power was on the side of the lay people. Ordinary citizens, even Christians, always develop their groups, ambitions, and rivalries. The business class does not see things in the same way as low-wage earners; men are aggressive, wives are fearful; the ignorant often become loudmouths and want to dominate the discussion. Underlying all of this is the consideration that American parochial schools attach a financial burden on the whole parish that supports them. Many people have problems with this. Nevertheless, the project inched along thanks to countless meetings in the rectory and never-ending public gatherings, that were either stormy or boring, but rarely constructive. Father Garin was too astute and experienced to tread these muddy pathways. He waited for the ground to harden under foot for a firmer stance. He prayed, he was patient, and ministered to everyone with such zeal that he gained thousands of friends. When the opponents became scarce enough to carry little weight, he acted. By December 1879, a beautiful large school began to take shape, measuring 94 by 45 feet. It had eight spacious classrooms and was completed in time for the start of the 1880-1881 school year.[31]

Father Garin at first thought of entrusting this school to the Sisters of the Holy Family of Bordeaux. But out of deference to the archbishop, who was not keen on bringing nuns from Europe, the Lowell priests unanimously agreed to seek the Gray Nuns of Ottawa. Eight nuns reported to their classrooms on Monday, September 6. At most 450 children were expected, but 550 showed up on opening day, and more than 600 by mid-September. The excellent impression made by the Sisters set the groundwork for a firm start. The young Immaculate Conception Parish, with its magnificent church, flanked by its Catholic school of nearly 1,000 students, could justly stand alongside the best America had to offer.

Former St. Jean Baptiste Church
Now Nuestra Senoira del Carman

Former St. Joseph Boy's School

CHAPTER NINE
ST. JOSEPH AND ST. JEAN-BAPTISTE CHURCHES

The construction of the Immaculate Conception Church and school in Lowell had absorbed Father Garin for eleven years from 1869 to 1880. Unbelievably, during the same general period, he found the means to build two other churches and organize many supplemental associations. These projects were not mentioned previously so that the historical narration of the Immaculate Conception Church could be presented as a whole. The time has now come to give special attention to Father Garin's achievements for the French Canadians of Lowell.

Already in 1868, as we have seen, he bought a former Protestant temple and converted it into a church for the exclusive use of the French Canadian Catholics. For two years, no major alterations were made to the structure. However, considerable changes were taking place in the Canadian colony. It increased by one fourth in only one year. Needless to say, adjustments were imperative in God's house to accommodate this wave of immigrants. Father Garin began by removing a partition in the lobby, thus gaining one hundred additional seats, but he could foresee that lofts would have to be added before long.[1]

His premonition came about sooner than expected. By the end of October, galleries were in place.[2] It was, however, a stopgap measure; a more ambitious and radical solution became a necessity. Father Garin cast his eyes on two small houses near the church and began to draw sketches. He made it known to everyone that he had no "architectural" purpose in mind, all he wanted was more space and shelter for those who came to Mass.[3] Matters understandably dragged. It's not easy to buy out a well-established neighbor who is not eager to sell and who is not even thinking of giving up a comfortable, pleasant home in a congenial location. Still, at the end of 1872,[4] Father Garin was the owner of the two small houses and construction began the following summer. No one was surprised when he hired Mr. Keely as the architect, the slow but very competent draftsman who forever became his right-hand man. This time the wind was blowing favorably. Mr. Keely caused no delay in the construction. By November 10, the parishioners were provided with a church measuring 83 square feet and seating 1,000 persons.[5] Father Joseph Mangin could say that the building had a pleasant aspect about it[6] The church was the property of the archbishop of Boston until 1887, at which time he ceded it outright to the Oblates.

In 1880, more improvements were undertaken that enlarged the church to 150 feet in length,[7] a change that pleased Father J. McGrath, then superior of the Lowell community.[8] The work was completed in 1881 and Archbishop Williams blessed the new church on May 21. On this festive occasion Archbishop Edward Fabre of Montreal celebrated the Mass, and Bishop Thomas Duhamel of Ottawa preached the sermon in French.[9] The church was now one of the largest religious buildings in the city, with a seating capacity of two thousand people.[10]

In spite of successive expansions, St. Joseph's church always remained inadequate, if we are to believe Father Louis Gladu, a young Oblate priest. He complained to the provincial on June 10, 1882, that of 11,000 Canadians in Lowell, only 5,000 attended Mass on Sunday. This was possibly an over-statement, in a rather churlish letter. For example, he felt that the Irish received much more attention, etc...[11] We surmise that Father Garin did not share that opinion, since he waited another seven long years before seeking improvements. He more than anybody loved his cherished Franco-Americans.

At the outset of 1889, the 2,000-seat church finally did prove inadequate for the needs of the Canadian colony. The pastor likewise noticed that the French-speaking population tended to settle in "Little Canada," a district about ten blocks from the church, along the Merrimack river. The obvious solution was to build a church for them in that section. To everyone else, such a plan was unthinkable. How could he bring his archbishop, his superiors, and the people to accept this audacious project? But, gifted with inde-finable charisma, he managed to obtain a compliant "yes" from all sides. The groundwork was laid and construction began on the beautiful and spacious St. Jean-Baptiste Church for the French-speaking immigrants.[12]

While the church was being built, a large hall on the top floor of the French school (which will be discussed later) was used temporarily for services. It could accommodate 500 persons.[13] Eventually, the new church began to emerge from the ground. The crypt was just about completed by the end of 1889. Father Garin happily informed Father Joseph Antoine, the assistant general, of this fact on November 14, and added that they had begun the plastering that same day.[14]

The construction work proceeded smoothly. The lower church[15] was opened for worship on February 2, 1890.[16] Father Celestin Augier, provincial of Canada, gave the homily. Bishop Isidore Clut O.M.I of Canada's Far North presided.[17] The lower level of the new church was acknowledged as the most beautiful in Lowell. Everything was there: a marble altar, stained glass windows, rich vestments and sacred vessels. The latter were gifts from Father Antoine himself.[18]

The Oblates now possessed two great French churches in Lowell. During the first year they registered 683 baptisms and 210 marriages. Although they had numbered 1,200 only twenty years previously, the Canadian population had now increased to 16,000 people.

The lower church would serve for a few years, but Father Garin could not be satisfied with that arrangement for very long. He assumed the task of the upper church in 1893, but as he was getting along in years,[19] the direction of the project was passed on to Father Mangin. The work went on until 1896. The completed church was blessed on December 13 of that year with Bishop Albert Pascal OMI as the speaker of the day.[20]

The Romanesque church faces the street with a monumental facade dominated by a large rose window framed in stone. A wide portico reaches down at the front. The one expansive nave is without transepts. Inside, the church reveals elegant pillars, crowned with sculptured capitals, and spacious lofts. Paintings framed with architectural moldings run the length of the walls. Everything sustains an aura of grandeur that is a credit to those who brought it to completion.[21] The churches of St. Jean-Baptiste and St. Joseph would meet the needs of the French-speaking population until 1904. At that time, it became necessary for the diocese to establish another parish, St. Louis de France, in Centralville.[22]

These churches were very much alive, with intense ministry and well-organized pastoral structures. It was the era of devotional societies such as the Ladies of Saint Anne for married women, Our Lady of Lourdes for the young ladies, the Children of Mary for the little girls who had made their first communion. Married men could belong to the society of the Holy Family, which also had a section for unmarried young men, and the society of the Guardian Angel for boys under 16.[23]

Father Garin also founded the C.M.A.C. an association for the "advancement and social development of the French population." At the beginning, it was made up of members of the Guardian Angel society and was known as the Young People's Catholic Action of St. Joseph's Parish. It was affiliated with the Young Men's Union.[24] In 1889 the association changed its constitution to admit married men, and became the Society for Mutual Assistance. Two years later, it was recognized by the State of Massachusetts as an insurance society, and incorporated under the acronym C.M.A.C.(Corporation des Membres de l'Association Catholique).[25] Another social enterprise was the Saint Andre Corporation, so named in honor of Father Andre Garin. It was a mutual society providing financial aid to its members in times of illness or death[26]

It's not surprising that Father Garin underscored in a letter to Father Antoine on June 20, 1898 that St. Jean-Baptiste Church had such a large attendance. Of the 1,200 seats, 900 were rented. Even so there was no change at St. Joseph's Church. It continued to be filled to capacity. The priests were overburdened. Seven of them were expected to meet the needs of the two churches, and the 16,000 French Canadians living in Lowell. For his part, Father Garin must now limit his activities. He no longer presided at High Mass, and did not take sick calls at night because, as he said, "I am no longer a young man."[27] He was now 71.

In spite of his assertions, he remained young at heart. He would have loved to do a great deal more. He deplored the fact that in Lowell the Oblates were constantly refusing requests for parish missions. This refusal was seen as a betrayal of the very purpose of their foundations on American soil.[28] However, he finally boasted that the establishments in Lowell were the most beautiful in the whole Oblate Congregation, anywhere in the world. With increased personnel, they could even set up a juniorate, a novitiate, and a scholasticate."[29]

Such was Father Garin's enthusiasm at the summit of his life. But now we need to backtrack. Hardly anything was said up to this point about his involvement in education, except with Immaculate Conception School. The time has come to consider other important endeavors.

The lack of French schools for French-Canadian students sorrowed him very deeply. He reflected at length about this problem, prayed over it, tried to find a way, and kept a finger up for a propitious wind. Until he could do better, he organized an evening school in 1876 that was attended by 800 boys and girls.

After the enlargement of St. Joseph Church, in 1881, Father McGrath admitted to Father Garin that the French parish needed to add a school like the one at Immaculate Conception.[30] It was a step forward, not to say a conversion, for he had shown little encouragement until then. In fact, at the beginning of the year he had hinted to the provincial that this project might not be timely. He cited financial problems.[31] He even shared his suspicion that Father Garin might be working underhandedly and shoring up arguments. Father McGrath noted that Father Garin usually marshaled his arguments with such vigor that they could not be easily refuted.

As the Lowell superior had foreseen, the proposal came to the provincial without delay. In June, Father Garin requested schools, and he wanted them immediately. The site had already been selected and there were several advantages to the project. A good business transaction was available on land that would perhaps be difficult to find later. They had to purchase the property immediately, and open a few classes in September. Father McGrath objected, considering the proposal Utopian. Mother Phelan, superior general of the Gray Nuns of Ottawa, had explained during her visit to Lowell that she did not have enough nuns.[32]

Father McGrath held the advantage for the time being, but on December 13, 1881, the local council of the Lowell Oblate residence reevaluated the problem. The first question they addressed concerned lodgings for the nuns. They proposed grouping all the Sisters of Lowell in one residence, at Immaculate Conception, of course. Father Garin objected that this did not make sense. The Sisters teaching at the St. Jean-Baptiste School would have to travel for twenty minutes, which would not be very inspirational on stormy days when the street cars were packed with people during the busiest hours. And furthermore, they would have to be content with a meager lunch at noon, since the school would be devoid of kitchen and dining hall. What an advantage it would be for them to have a separate house: their own residence with a small garden.

All agreed on the site and plan for the school. The council voted unanimously to open a few classes in September 1882, and then to have a complete school by the following September.[33] Father McGrath was horrified by the proposed budget. The cost of the building was estimated at $35,000, excluding the nun's house, which meant a minimum expenditure of $40,000 in all. Since the Oblate residence was already $45,000 in debt, they faced a total debt of $85,000.[34] Contributions for the school proved a fiasco: they had yielded only $1,710 to date. Father McGrath concluded that a wooden school should be built instead of a brick structure. He expected that such a building would cost only $20,000 and could last 25 to 30 years. The City of Lowell, certainly richer than the Oblates, already had several such schools.[35]

Father McGrath's plan, although more economical than Father Garin's, had one major flaw. It gave the impression that the French people were being relegated to a second class status, although they were the main reason why the Oblates came to Lowell.

Father Garin did not budge an inch and he finally won his case. A large, four-story brick school building measuring 85 by 70 feet was erected on Moody Street. The Gray Nuns of the Cross contracted to teach girls and boys up to the age of twelve. Father Garin himself had gone to Ottawa and had recruited eight nuns from Mother Phelan. The nuns arrived in Lowell on October 26, 1883, but since their house was not yet finished, they lived in the Immaculate Conception convent until November 7. The following week, the school finally opened its doors to a student body of 490 boys and 300 girls.[36]

The opening of the school year in this impressive $50,000 building was observed with great solemnity. After Mass at the church, the children marched through the major streets of the city. According to Father Garin they should walk openly for all to see. He led the triumphal march himself, having once remarked from the pulpit: "If you do not see Father Garin in the street on that day you may pray for him, because it would mean that he is very sick." The parade startled many of Lowell's citizens. They could not believe that the city really included that many Franco-American children.[37] But Father Garin's regiment of school children was not made up entirely of angels. It included a number of incorrigible rascals, transferred from the public schools. The police complained, rightly or wrongly, about numerous pranks after classes. Some of the young scholars went as far as knocking over trash barrels as they passed in front of private residences.[38]

This first French school in Lowell, and probably in the whole archdiocese of Boston, grew rapidly. In September 1887, 1,300 students attended the Mass of the Holy Spirit, 500 more than when the school first opened. Father Garin then purchased another building at 510 Moody Street which became known as "the Little White School." It was able to accept about one hundred boys from seven to ten years of age.[39] When the Members of the Lowell School Committee came to inspect the whole complex, they stated that the city could not surpass what was going on here.[40]

The French-Canadian children were indeed privileged, but Father Garin set his sights a bit higher. He wanted each group, boys and girls, to have their own school. He noticed a superb brick building that was available and hurriedly wrote to Father Antoine on November 14, 1889: "Undoubtedly, this would provide us with the most elegant facility of its kind in all of the New England States."[41] After a few months of negotiation, however, this wonderful project fell through. It would cost too much.[42] Father finally decided to build elsewhere and would have reason to be more pleased at the outcome.[43] On land that was nearly facing St. Jean-Baptiste Church, he was able to erect a huge building 104 by 56 feet, which consisted of fifteen classrooms and two large halls. On September 3, 1892, eight Marist Brothers came to direct this imposing facility.[44] The founder was extremely happy. His two schools now had more than 1,800 students.[45]

What more can be said about Father Garin's activities? As a good shepherd, he thought of everyone, even the deceased. It grieved him to see the dead buried haphazardly in the large anonymous public cemeteries. He believed in the compassionate tradition of the family plot in consecrated ground, where loved ones rested in peace. Parents and friends could then visit the graves of their beloved. The parish cemetery is not just a sentiment; it is a church institution and part of parish life. Father Garin felt this deeply. Practical as always, when nothing moved, he intervened, took the initiative and acted. The death of Father Christophe Phaneuf in 1872 supplied the occasion.[46] A small plot of land was needed in which to bury the deceased Oblate. The Lowell superior bought a huge tract, in expectation of future development. The final arrangements for the cemetery were completed in 1893, two years before receiving the venerable remains of the beloved founder.[47]

As a good superior, Father Garin always gave high priority to the concerns of his community. He and his Oblates had their first lodgings at St. John's Hospital, and later, in a small house shared with other tenants. The place itself was not as suitable as he had initially thought. The thin walls were not impervious to all the noises from the neighboring flat. All too often, the woman next door practiced the piano while they were at evening meditation.[48] That explains his haste in acquiring a lot with two large houses on it, one of which would serve as a residence. But when the day came to form two separate Oblate communities, one for the Immaculate Conception and the other for St. Joseph, Father Garin selected a 20,000 square foot plot that contained a small, but admirable cottage built in the style of the area. This residence, the Bonney house, seemed to have been built expressly for a community of religious. He lost no time in buying it in 1887, and after some minor modifications, installed his happy religious family therein.[49] He served as Superior to the French priests for 6 years until 1893, the year he returned from a general meeting of the Oblates in Europe. He had previously been superior of the first community in Lowell from 1868 to 1874.

These pages have attempted to present, in summary form, the colossal task accomplished by Father Garin for the Franco-Americans of Lowell. He was certainly prophetic when he pressed for this foundation. He supported it unstintingly with his dynamic and compelling personality. If the works of the Oblates have lasted and are flourishing today, one must say that it was Father Garin who provided the inspiration and lit the initial spark. In Lowell, he deserves the stature of a true founder.

St. Joseph The Worker Shrine

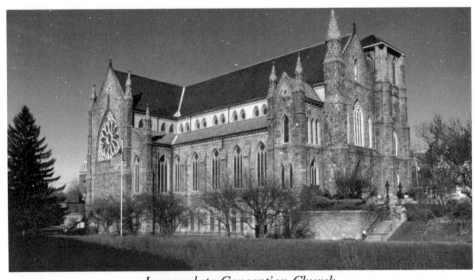
Immaculate Conception Church

CHAPTER TEN
VARIOUS WORKS

Preaching parish missions to the Canadians in the Boston and neighboring dioceses was one of the main reasons for the Lowell foundation. In spite of their restricted number, the priests always found a way to respond to this need. In 1868 we find them conducting missions in Lowell, Lawrence, Haverhill, West Boylston and Marlboro Massachusetts. In 1869 they traveled not only to Nashua New Hampshire and Webster, Gloucester, and Fitchburg Massachusetts, but also to the dioceses of Albany, Toronto, Erie, Kingston, Cleveland, etc. In 1870, the Oblates visited the dioceses of Albany, Cleveland, and Portland. In the city of Fall River alone, they distributed communion to 15,812 persons.[1] The demand for missions was growing enormously. In a report to the general administration on November 1, 1881, Father McGrath lists the cities and towns in which the fathers had preached since 1879. In that year they conducted missions in Lowell, Worcester, Brooklyn, St. Johnsbury, Plattsburgh, Ellsworth, and Exeter. In 1880 the list includes Hoboken, Boston, Portland, Concord, New York City, Newark, Renovo, East-Hampshire, Turner's Falls, and Suncook. In 1881, Providence, Middleton, Portland, Malone and Messina. Their activities had thus extended from the diocese of Boston to the dioceses of Portland, Burlington, Providence, Hartford, Springfield, New York, Brooklyn, Newark, and Harrisburg.[2]

Faced with this enormous task, and especially with the many requests that could not be fulfilled, the Lowell superiors constantly pleaded for additional missionaries. We have already heard Father Garin complain about the situation.

He was far from neglecting the French people in rural areas. Father Tortel, the author of Father Garin's obituary, wrote, "Our priests willingly traveled to Canadian groups at various times of the year, either to preach a mission or to allow them to accomplish their Easter duty. They also devised ingenious ways to erect chapels where they were needed.

"We point out in particular the centers at Nashua, Lawrence, Woburn, and Winchester. These chapels blossomed into beautiful Canadian parishes that owe their origin to the zeal and the skillful interventions of the Oblates, especially Father Garin. We are sure that several other Canadian groups learned from him how to go about getting a church and parish started. If ever a misunderstanding surfaced, such as happened in Fall River, the diocesan authority could call on the dedication and know-how of the true Father of the Canadians to soothe the minds and quell the scandal."[3]

Father Garin continuously insisted that the provincial provide help so that Canadian groups without a pastor could be reached. He emphasized this request forcefully when Archbishop Williams needed priests for Lawrence, a few short miles from Lowell.[4] Father Vandenberghe sought a priest in Ottawa, because he had no one available in Montreal.[5] Things dragged on, in spite of Father Garin's two pressuring letters in 1871. At first he requested Father Christophe Phaneuf[6], and a little later, insisted on a definite reply.[7] His plea was heard at last, and he could happily inform the archbishop that Father J. B. Baudin, would be coming. He would introduce him on December 5. This new appointment placed enormous hardships on the provincial. A few months later, he had to turn down a mission to St. Maurice, in Quebec, because of this. He gave the reason to Archbishop Baillargeon: "For two months our priests in Lowell have been providing regular services in two important cities, Lawrence and Haverhill, in order to ready the people for a permanent congregation. In Lawrence, the Canadians are in sufficient numbers to maintain a priest. All we can do currently is merely acknowledge those other areas where the Canadians are few in number."[8]

Father Garin kept a close watch on Father Baudin's work. After having spoken highly of him in a letter to the provincial on December 29, he reported on March 22 that the priest had just purchased a Protestant temple and would be transforming it into a Catholic church. The nascent work was beginning to bear fruit. Unfortunately, the pastor's appointment came to its term. He left Lowell on April 9, and was replaced by Father Phidime Lecompte who stayed in Lawrence until mid-September 1872.

In the provincial's mind, Lawrence was only a temporary post, and Father Garin was clearly reminded of this fact. Father Garin responded that if that was the case, the Oblates should take it upon themselves to find a good Canadian priest to continue the work.[9] He found one himself, in the person of Father M. J. Michaud, who served the parish until 1878. At his departure, Archbishop Williams again wanted to entrust the new post to the Oblates. Father Garin immediately informed Father Vandenberghe. He implored the Provincial to allow Father Lecompte to return to Lawrence and again serve the Canadians until they could find a priest to satisfy the needs of the archdiocese. This prayer, it seems, was not granted.

Despite their short stay in Lawrence, the Oblates did very fine work, thanks to Father Garin. James Sullivan mentions him in his History of the Archdiocese of Boston. While relating the events that we have covered, Sullivan attributed most of the credit to Father Garin since both Fathers Baudin and Lecompte, had resided in Lowell under his immediate jurisdiction.[10]

It was a different story at St. Andrew's Church in Billerica.[11] The priests worked there for many years, from 1868 to 1913. A small group of Irish people needed a priest in that town. Father Garin again pleaded with his superiors in favor of Archbishop Williams by asking for an Oblate post. He said that to serve this small mission would be in the Oblates' best interest. The priest who served this modest mission could preach retreats in the neighboring cities and towns on alternate Sundays. The Provincial remained reticent and delayed his reply. After some mild harassment Father Garin, put into practice the principle "He who is silent consents." He accepted the post in the name of the Oblates. Father Louis Lebret was placed in charge. The church was blessed on November 15, 1868, under the patronage of Saint Andrew. No doubt, this was a reference to Father Andre Garin's patron saint.

In 1878, again at Father Garin's urging, the Oblates began to minister at the City Farm, or Poor House, in Tewksbury. This establishment sheltered the elderly, and the mentally ill. It also included a section for maternity. This kind of ministry came well within the scope of the Oblate Congregation. This is confirmed in Father Vandenberghe's report of February 2, 1872, to Father Joseph Fabre, the superior general.

On the subject of Tewksbury, he wrote, "Father MacKernan spends the whole day there every Tuesday, and is called back whenever someone is sick. On average, there are between five hundred and six hundred poor people, two thirds of whom are Catholic. There are no regular religious services because the State will not allow them. Our ministry is not financially reimbursed. It is a worthy cause where much good can be done."[12] With the passing of time, the pastoral services became more regular and more demanding. In 1881, the buildings housed 950 unfortunate residents. Father Frederic Gigault, the chaplain, visited them several times a week.

When the American Province was organized, Tewksbury was chosen as the site for a novitiate. Bishop Healy dedicated the building on October 28, 1883, and it began receiving novices on November 10th.[13] In 1888, a juniorate was added, but it was transferred to Buffalo in 1892.[14] Again, Father Garin's initiatives in Tewksbury were to benefit the Province.

Apparently the multitude of these engrossing works never diminished his enthusiasm. His superiors still called on him for delicate missions. For example, he was sent to Savannah, Georgia, for an on-sight study of a proposed establishment. In 1867, Bishop Augustin Verot of Savannah beseeched the Oblates to take charge of a parish that was reaching out to evangelize the blacks in Georgia. He went to Montreal hoping to speed up the negotiations. Father Joseph Tabaret made the project known to the superior general on May 3, 1867: "Bishop Verot, of Savannah, arrived here yesterday morning. This good bishop came specifically to ask for missionaries. I sent Father Garin to Savannah a month ago to study the situation there. His report corroborates the information we had already received." Although the Oblates wished to expand throughout the United States, this offer seemed incompatible with their present situation.[15] Father Garin's judgment appears to have been influential in the final decision.

Others must have noticed his southern tour. On January 4, 1873, Bishop W. H. Cross, CSSR, not knowing where to write, addressed Father Garin requesting missionaries for Georgia. The Lowell priest again relayed the message to the provincial who had to refuse due to the lack of personnel.

In 1884, Father Garin was approached once more, this time regarding a projected foundation in New York City.[16] This request was also turned down. Father considered it more advantageous to take firm root in Lowell than to think of expansion. He cannot be blamed, in the light of the tremendous development taking place there, with such a limited number of workers. Events bore him out. Thanks to his initiative, on June 6, 1870, the Oblates took root on American soil when the State of Massachusetts granted them a legal decree of civil incorporation under the name of The Society of Oblate Fathers for Missions among The Poor.

CHAPTER ELEVEN
THE "BON PERE"

Father Garin's many accomplishments won him everlasting fame. But his dedication, fervor, and kindly manners earned him the endearing title of "Bon Pere," "Good Father." It was by this name that his parishioners and admirers knew him.

Father Garin's kindness revealed itself in deeds of delicate thoughtfulness. Mother Bruyere, Superior General of the Gray Nuns, who had a fine knowledge of people, wrote to Sister Phelan during a visit to her nuns in Plattsburgh on November 5, 1860: "As to this Father (Garin), I must say that he is exceedingly kind...He has even provided us with the food to celebrate this occasion." On November 8, she wrote again, "Reverend Father Garin is truly good in spiritual matters as well as temporal, and he takes good care of our Sisters. Would you believe that last Monday he was kind enough to attend the instruction given to us by Father Aubert? He came on his own initiative. That pleased me very much because it gives us the hope that he intends to continue along the same paths as our good Father Aubert."[2]

As she was leaving for Buffalo, Sister Lavoie wrote to Mother Bruyere: "Your short grief does not seem to appreciate our loss in the person of our Father Garin ...We have been spoiled since we came here. That is why this sacrifice is so painful for us."[3]

In the annals of the Plattsburgh convent, the recorder wrote unequivocally: "On November 2, our Father Garin came to bid farewell to the community. Each of our Sisters completely felt all that the Plattsburgh residence was losing by the departure of the one who brought us here. Since the arrival of our Sisters in this city, he has always shown limitless interest and faithfulness. We could never show enough gratitude to this good Father, because such kind hearted men are rarely encountered."[4]

Archbishop Williams, in his own fashion, praised the fathers when he met Father Soulier, a canonical visitor, in 1876. "Your Oblates work very hard and cause no trouble to their bishop."[5] We can add that this was due to Father Garin's leadership. He troubled no one, hurt no one. That was his policy and his constant preoccupation. He radiated this policy around him, and made it the motto for his whole community.

In the mind of the people, Father Garin belonged to the group called "Les Saints Peres", "the holy Fathers." The necrology of a Lowell priest reads in part: "From the advent of the holy Fathers in Lowell, the good and not so good said to themselves that compassion and forgiveness had chosen to make their abode in this city. All those troubled with physical or moral anguish could now find refuge in the presence of the good Fathers."[6] As we can see, Father Garin's spirit and mentality became the hallmark of his religious community. In 1876, Father Norbert Ouellette noted in his written response during a canonical visitation, that Father Garin heard confessions of as many Irish as he did of Canadians. His mercy was well known and could leap over many parochial boundaries. The same priest added that when the local citizenry referred to St. Joseph's Church, they simply called it "Father Garin's Church."[7]

Father Ouellette was not the only one to speak so favorably of the Lowell superior. In the course of a speech delivered upon his arrival in Lowell during October 1898, Father Joseph Lefebvre said: "The good and sadly mourned Father Garin, the first shepherd, became that good and faithful steward referred to in Sacred Scripture. He eventually transformed Lowell with the zealous works inspired by his genial talent. Honor is due to him and to the co-workers who assisted him. Honor is equally due to this responsive and intelligent population, that did not hesitate to show its esteem, its filial affection, its gratitude. We remember the magnificent celebration of his golden jubilee, the truly unforgettable funeral, and finally, the splendid monument, erected to perpetuate his memory and his steadfast devotion for generations to come.

"I said his steadfast devotion. In fact, from 1868 when he arrived in your midst, until 1895, a span of 27 years, he never for an instant stopped working in your behalf. Let me recall a minor, but important, incident. It proves that nothing that affected you escaped his solicitude. When he first came to Lowell, not many Americans knew French. None of the employees at the Post Office spoke our language. Consequently, many letters remained undelivered. What did the good priest do? He struck an arrangement with the Post Office that all letters to the Canadians be delivered to him. He held mail-call in the church, and was a little mischievous with the few who had Anglicized their name. Thus did he render unique services to his parishioners."[8]

"His rare common sense," further observed Father Tortel, "his prudent patience, his practical knowledge of people and things that stemmed from strong powers of observation, his charming frankness with everyone, particularly with his people, his noble simplicity of manners, his superbly resonant and sympathetic voice, all of these together generated a congruence of traits that quickly and unquestionably established his authority in the minds and hearts of the parishioners of St. Joseph's Church.

"Let us point out, in the interest of truth, that his approach to people was not in the formal content of his sermons. His humble baggage of oratory consisted of a few mission sermons and orations for formal occasions. He led his parish by informal announcements from the pulpit. His counsels and unpretentious commentaries were in the tradition of the early Oblates, who drew the secret of their successful missions from the same well. This type of simple preaching, familiar, but never trivial, enabled him to carry out his true calling. His fatherly guidance reached out indiscriminately to individuals and families, present or absent. His words did not fall on barren ground; they were repeated by the parishioners as the news of the day. 'Have you heard what Father Garin announced?' Did you catch his advice?' This was the tone of conversations during the week. People were waiting impatiently for more advice or some interesting development on the following Sunday. Many times when the assistant priests were visiting families, they heard the Canadian mothers exclaim to their children: 'Now, watch out. You know what Father Garin said.'

"Ever the vigilant sentry with open eyes and ears, he would mull over what he observed from Monday to Saturday and then, at times just before mounting the pulpit, decided which pitfall to expose for the protection of his flock. How many parties, wild ventures, and dances,[9] how many pleasure trips which the newspapers advertised in large print, but were devoid of spiritual or sensible benefit, came to a halt before one of Father Garin's announcements! His astute mind could lend itself to all tones: soft or trenchant, solemn or familiar, grave or pleasant, with a note of sympathy as the dominant. Whoever heard him, for better or worse, could not forget him. It must be said, however, that his early preaching did not always go over too well because some of his references were too transparent and personal. He had the good sense to realize this, and corrected it by taking a softer approach.

"His method of preaching, once adjusted, remained on target, to everyone's benefit for twenty-seven years. The influence never diminished, even though the number of immigrants doubled and even tripled each year. If one person left, two or three arrived. This increase did demand more work, but the stalwarts among the older Franco-American citizens maintained a respect for Christian morality that influenced the general population. The people could then be kept alert with the stirrings of the annual and Lenten missions."[10]

In the midst of his countless projects, Father Garin remained the apostle for all. Each year he had his personal contingent of Protestant converts. He also had the knack of arousing extraordinary acts of generosity from the

people of Lowell for the construction of churches and schools. He was so
well acquainted with the establishment of parishes that he could say: "If you
want the parishioners to appreciate the devotion of their priest, ask them to
contribute generously to both the priest and the church."[11] His success is
well known. "One must take the weather as it comes, the people as they are,
and money when it is available...I refused some once," he added with a
smile, "and I learned to regret it. A man came to me one day to pay for his
pew rental. I was very busy, so I told him to return the next day. He never
came back."[12]

Father Garin's great kindness made him the least complicated of men.
Whenever he spoke to his superiors about his successes or his works, he did
so with the naturalness and candor of a child. He said to the superior general: "If I have not served the Oblate Congregation through my virtues as
much as I should have, I believe I have accomplished something for it to be
proud of. The good Lord used me to set up our establishment in Lowell.
You have heard of it, you know it. Perhaps I am a little too proud of it, but
I believe the good Lord will forgive me that pride, because all I had in mind
was the glory of God and the welfare of our Congregation, which I love and
will always love as a mother."[13]

Even to the end of his life, he kept that same simplicity of soul and child-
like heart. At the grand banquet celebrating his golden anniversary, he said
quite simply in response to the complimentary speeches, "It is true, I have
loved my Congregation! I have had to bear hardships and many labors, but
never did the least feeling of discouragement enter my heart. I say this with
gratitude to God. The Congregation has always been a good mother to me,
so I could never find a reason to withhold my love. The thought of leaving
never occurred to me. When it suffered, I also suffered; when it rejoiced, I
equally rejoiced."[14]

Father Garin loved his Congregation in its superiors, and above all in its
Superior General, Father Joseph Fabre. At the latter's death, he wrote to
Father J. E. Antoine in Paris: "Let us acknowledge that if I have done some
wrongful deeds in my life, I have done some good ones also, one of which
was attracting this man to the Congregation."[15]

We can now understand Father Garin's acquiescence, towards the end of
his life, when Father Soulier, the superior general, wrote to tell him that
Father Avila Amyot would replace him as head of the community. His
response is worth quoting, for it is one of the best examples we can find of
noble religious spirit. The general's letter was only handed over to him on
his return to Lowell. The provincial, Father McGrath, gave it to him in person. The good man, he wrote later, "wanted me to enjoy my triumphs in

peace."[16] He continued: "But be that as it may, I received and read your letter with the proper emotions that one with 51 years of religious vows should have. I kissed your letter respectfully, and went to see Reverend Father Amyot who was totally embarrassed in his humility. I told him he could count on my good will to help him no matter where or when. The new provincial came in the afternoon to install Father Amyot as superior of the St. Joseph residence. This was followed by the most pleasant of suppers...Everything continues to run perfectly, as if nothing had happened. All the Fathers are quite satisfied and so am I."[17]

There can be no doubt that this change affected Father Garin somewhat deeply. It was an obvious sign that his career was coming to an end. He had been on the provincial council, and was just returning from the general chapter which he had attended as a delegate of the fathers in the province. Finally, he was able to contain his disappointment without displaying the least sign of moodiness.

Father Garin's Superiors were unreserved in their esteem for him because his great gentleness was based on energy and solidity. In his canonical visit of 1876, Father Soulier spoke highly of the religious discipline which the superior maintained in his house. And this is only in corroboration of an 1872 provincial document which praised Father Garin's community very highly for its fine behavior and exemplary dedication. It was unified, working, and productive. The routine was ideal: a daily schedule adapted to the needs of the ministry. There was no abuse of absences, household visits, or personal projects. Charity reigned within and without. Unity of hearts lingered under the diversity of work and opinions.

Throughout this report, all of Father Garin's stewardship was made manifest. The provincial added, in his words to the general, "Father superior is known to you...He practices and imposes religious poverty. His piety is not showy but nonetheless firm. His love for the congregation is generally known."[18] To the gentle and to the peaceful, that is to say the meek at heart, the Gospel promises that they shall inherit the earth. In other words, they will win over the hearts of people. This phenomenon took place in Lowell. Father Garin's flock loved him with a respect that amounted to veneration.

All of this was obvious at the celebration of his fiftieth anniversary of religious life. It was an extraordinary triumph. The entire city honored a hero, and the parishioners of St. Joseph's, a father and a friend. A parade was organized the likes of which Lowell may never have seen. All the parish societies marched by, along with many from outside the area. Father Garin had to resign himself to the outpouring of praises from all these groups. The days of the celebration were exhausting, but how uplifting for him. He revealed his joy in a letter to Father Antoine, "The observance of my religious jubilee was splendid. I rejoiced in the occasion because it brought great honor to our religion in the eyes of Americans."

He added that on November 6, he was presented with a gift of more than $6,000. The old taskmaster had every right to be proud. The grand mission of his life was emerging as a success. Everyone acknowledged it, even Father Aime Martinet, a canonical visitor and reputed to be the least excitable of men. He exclaimed, "How unfortunate that Father General himself cannot be here to see all this. He is so appreciative of things that are well done."[19] As always, Father Garin acknowledged the compliment honestly and without pride, but he wanted to be sure that his Oblate conferers, who remained in the shadows, were not forgotten. In November 1884, at the solemn celebration of his patronal feast day he responded to the many praises of his virtues and accomplishments by saying: "My dear friends, it is now time, as the Canadians say, to 'tirer ses comptes', to set the accounts straight. You say in your speeches that it is I who have created and founded everything in this parish. When we straighten out the accounts you will find that poor Father Garin, after all, had but a rather small part in all this."[20] The real founders of St. Joseph's Parish are the Fathers Lucien Lagier, Adolphe Tortel, Basile Dedebant, Louis Gladu, Louis Petit, Charles Lagier, Athanase Marion, and Joseph Fournier.

A gift of Stations of the Cross for the church was presented to him on this occasion. His reaction was that after his death, good Catholics would think: "That poor Father Garin who baptized us, married us, and often talked to us in his sermons about the souls suffering in purgatory is perhaps there himself. Let's offer the Stations of the Cross for his intention...There may be rumors that perhaps these Stations of the Cross were given to me as symbols of the sufferings that I had to bear in this community. Oh, but no! The road to Calvary is strewn with brambles and thorns, but the road on which I traveled here was enclosed with roses and flowers. From the bottom of my heart, I can say that the seventeen years I spent among you were the most beautiful of my life."[21]

The beloved priest was right. Few pastors were more loved by their people. There was a triumphal reception for "le Bon Pere" upon his return from the General Chapter in 1893. A delegation of distinguished citizens journeyed to New York to welcome him at the dock. He describes his arrival in Lowell: "A detachment of Lowell 'policemen' were there to receive me." The pastor then had to resign himself to a lengthy procession through the streets of his broad parish. People crowded together all along the way, interrupting the parade to cheer their beloved pastor.

Was there ever any criticism from some parishioners? It could not be otherwise. One elder parishioner wrote of his experience, and its outcome: "I was critical at certain times of the way he administered parish affairs, but considering today the great works he accomplished, I see that I was wrong. If I had understood him then, I would not have acted as I did."[22]

The author of Father Garin's obituary notice, after portraying a life bursting with activity, went on to say without hesitation, "Beneath that brilliant and consuming activity was concealed an inner spiritual source that animated everything. It was the heart of a true Oblate which drew its energy, even at the scholasticate, directly from the heart of our saintly founder. This contact with Bishop Eugene de Mazenod was the source of a deep fidelity to his apostolic vocation, as it was for all the early fathers who shared the same experience. Reverend Father Garin took a saintly pride in his religious family and shared deeply in its joys and its sorrows.

"His piety was sustained by a complete trust in the authority of the Rule and in its merit. He strayed from it as little as possible in his personal behavior, and in the guidance of his community. If he did stray, it was through weakness, never defiance. All who lived with him during his long career can testify that from five o'clock in the morning to nine-thirty at night, he was usually faithful to the community exercises. It was there that he found spiritual nourishment for each day. He especially enjoyed the communal recitation of the breviary.

"His sense of religious poverty brought him to a sort of saintly indifference. He cared little about his personal appearance, and wore garments given to him until they were threadbare. It went beyond what would normally be acceptable. Like Bishop Guigues, for many years he kept a light winter coat that was inverted, reversed, or dyed as needed. At the beginning of each winter, the citizens living along fashionable Merrimack Street would go to their windows when he was passing by to enjoy the appearance of the famous 'coat' and then engage the wearer in friendly banter.[23]

"Only a few who were close to him were aware that for the last forty years his cheerful mood and playful words concealed a sad and often painful affliction, probably contracted during his missions to the Indians. It took the form of a skin disease that itched and gnawed, heated the blood, and continuously produced sores over his entire body. The least scratch drew blood. He endured this sort of hairshirt bravely, and kept his discomfort unknown to most."[24]

The brief portrait we have presented reveals the rich and noble character of a man who earned the beautiful and simple title of "le Bon Pere."

CHAPTER TWELVE
THE FINAL TRIUMPH

Early in 1893, the general chapter of the Oblates gathered to elect a successor to Father Joseph Fabre who had died on October 26, 1892. Father Garin was chosen as the delegate of the American province at this important meeting. He took advantage of this European voyage to visit the parish of his birth and celebrate fifty years of religious life.[1]

Once he was back in Lowell, his plan, as formulated in Europe, was to complete the construction of St. Jean-Baptiste Church. Then he would return to prepare for death in the shadow of the beloved shrine of Notre Dame de l'Osier, which had inspired his youthful religious life. God had other plans, however. His life would cease in the theater of his labors.

Father Garin resumed his work on the church, but only for a short time. During February of 1895, he was stricken with a fever that the physician did not consider dangerous at the moment. He was even able to receive visits from his friends. One was an Episcopalian minister who esteemed him very highly.[2] In his usual bantering tone, he suddenly asked the minister point blank, "Have you come to hear my confession?"

"I will be happy to oblige, if need be," the reverend replied.

"No," continued the invalid, "I do not believe I am in danger right now, but if my condition worsens I will let you know."

The moment arrived, however, when banter gave way to concern. He was taken to St. John's Hospital, his first home in Lowell. The Daughters of Charity of St. Vincent de Paul had not forgotten the one who had presided at Mass for them every morning for some twenty years. Father Garin then offered his life as a sacrifice to God. He also offered the church which he regretted not having the time to finish. The viaticum was administered on February 14. His next request was to be vested with the scapular of the Congregation. When someone tried to slide it under his garments, he protested,"No, no, all on the outside." He wished to die with the insignia of his religious family well in evidence, like a soldier who refuses to give up his weapons. The Oblates kept a vigil during the night of February 15 to 16. On that day he commended his soul to God, at the age of 73.

The news stunned the parish. "Our Father is dead," could be heard everywhere. St. Jean-Baptiste Church was completely filled during the whole time that the body could be viewed. An estimated 30,000 people filed past his open casket.[3]

Sorrow held the day in Lowell's two Oblate houses. The chronicler in the

St. Joseph residence reported: "The death of Reverend Father Garin made a profound impression in Lowell where he was well known and highly esteemed by all citizens, without distinction. All the city's newspapers expressed their regrets at his death and had only the highest praise for his work, zeal, and accomplishments."

The annals of the Immaculate Conception residence stated briefly, on February 16: "A great loss occurred today. Our dear old patriarch Rev. A. Garin passed away at St. John's Hospital at 7:30 a.m. today. Frs. Provincial, Nolin and Marion were with him at his departure. The local papers are so complete with his death notices that better cannot be done than insert them in the following pages."

The news must have spread like a trail of gunpowder. Even in Ottawa, on the same day, February 16, the annals of the Gray Nuns of the Cross include this entry: "This morning we learned of the death in Lowell of the good and revered Father Garin. This worthy Father was the founder of our Plattsburgh residence, and he also brought our Sisters to St. Joseph's Parish in Lowell. He always displayed a fatherly interest in our sisters, and he held the esteem, the trust, and the respectful affection of all the ones who knew him."

The day of Father Garin's funeral was as solemn as a national day of bereavement. Most of Lowell's business establishments closed their doors, and the streets through which the funeral cortege passed were draped in mourning. Photographs of the deceased were displayed in the windows of the stores.

Archbishop Williams insisted on presiding at the funeral ceremony, assisted by his coadjutor, Bishop Brady, and numerous clergy. Also present were the mayor of Lowell and all his council, an impressive number of distinguished citizens, and all of Lowell's French Canadian population. Never had such a crowd been seen at a funeral. The men of the parish societies alone numbered over 1,300. Father Joseph Lefebvre gave the funeral oration in French, and Father Daniel O'Riordon spoke in English. Both the Catholic and secular newspapers were unanimous in praising the character and the worthiness of the beloved departed. It was even suggested that a monument be erected in his honor. This became a reality on October 22, 1896, less than two years later. Lengthy extracts from the secular press are provided here because these testimonials are so much more impressive, coming from cultures that are often strangers to our faith.

The Lowell Sun[4] featured in large headlines: "REV. FR. GARIN, OMI IS DEAD" And in the sub-heading: "Like a little child he left this earth to receive his reward". And a third banner: "The Great French Catholic flock is

Left Without the Kindly Shepherd Who Has Led Them Many Years". Then the article: "The angel of death visited St. John's Hospital this morning, and claimed as its treasure the soul of Rev. Reverend Andre Garin, OMI, the most prominent Frenchman in this country. As the good sisters truly said the venerable priest passed away as he had lived, peacefully, happily and well prepared. It was on December 31st that Fr. Garin was admitted...He was conscious to the last and had often spoken, with a happy smile of his coming journey, home...Fr. Garin requested that his pillow be changed. The sister who was at his bedside attempted to raise him and he said in a weak voice: 'Don't try it, dear sister, I'm too heavy for your strength'.

"He died as he had wished, his work accomplished. He had said to the good sisters yesterday when the Angelus rang, 'I am going home.' and in the simplicity of his faith, and in fullness of years, his spirit was released from the mortal frame.

"The entire community is plunged in mourning; grief is not confined to the great flock of French Catholics to whom he was a shepherd; nor to the Catholics of the city at large; there is sincere sorrow among all, Protestants and non-church goers alike, that Death's hand should have taken from our midst one who shared the respect, love and friendship of the whole community. The French people have lost their best friend, his place will not be filled, if ever, for a long time, but his saintly character will remain a cherished memory."

Another newspaper, The Lowell Courier, said that in his last moments, Father Garin said to Father Daniel O'Riordon a very close friend: "Do not forget me." The account then mentions that Father O'Riordon "considered Fr. Garin the dearest friend the Irish people had in Lowell."

In describing a memorial service that was held later in Huntington Hall, The Lowell Daily News[5] quoted these words of Father Dacy, "The name of Garin -- 'twas a name to conjure by, -- none there were who dared to question when that name was employed. He was a ruler mighty in the land. He was a father, -- yes, but a heart as loving as a mother's beat within that father's breast. And what gave him this command, this power of ruling? It was not his great learning, and his knowledge of high and mighty things. 'Twas that wisdom that was founded in the fear of God...Better is wisdom than weapons of war. By his God-fearing wisdom he delivered his people from the enemies of his Holy Religion. He united them, made them strong, gave them the example of old, that as he had done so should they do likewise to each other.

"As an Oblate he was ever the sincere religious. He hated sham piety. He wished that all his brothers should be sincere, earnest religious. He was kindness itself in the community, ever looking for the happiness and comfort of the other members. His was not a querulous old age. It was an age of sunshine, and that sunshine lasted until the dark night of death closed around him and forever obscured the sun of his life. He went home joyfully, well satisfied that he had one his Master's will."

During that same ceremony, Philip Farley, an attorney, praised the role of Father Garin as a citizen and as a leader. His speech was reported in the above newspaper. He said, in part, "He spent the best years of his life among the Algonquin[7] and Iroquois; he came possessing all the grace and refinement of polished France; he had a temperament and a nobility of soul which in the service of the Most High made him one of nature's priests among men, and which, given free play under the benign influences of American institutions, made him a leader of his people and a superb citizen of the republic...

"And though in the long years he lived amongst us thousands of dollars passed through his hands, he died absolutely without wealth of any kind as though he had never controlled the expenditure of a cent. He made no will, because he had nothing to leave to any one. No heir of his will quarrel about his legacy, because the only one he left was the legacy of a holy life to his fellow priests, -- a life of sacrifice and labor and devotedness to his own people and to all us citizens of Lowell...

"He was the standard bearer of the helpless and the oppressed; his life was spent in the service of the poor and the uplifting of humanity; tolerance and liberality always marked his judgment of his fellow-men, their actions and their opinions; and hence no differences of religious belief separated the citizens of our city as they stood around his bier to pay their tribute to his worth and works...

"His was a life of sacrifice, as a passing glance at his labors will show...By his honesty and sincerity in every relation and office of his life, he won for himself a place in the hearts and affections of our people; and the citizens of Lowell, without regard to religious belief, mourn the great loss which the city has sustained in his death. He was preeminently the leader in our city of a people who today number twenty thousand of our population. Willingly and naturally they have adapted themselves to our form of government; they have brought with them to our community thrift, energy and perseverance, potent elements in the development of the highest type of American citizenship. To the honor of Fr. Garin, and to their credit be it said, among their number there are no socialists, communists or anarchists. They are an honest, God-fearing and liberty-loving people.

Weep, you, his people, for this gifted priest and leader; mourn, City of

Lowell, for the citizen that has passed away; and do you, oh, Catholics of the city, shower your tributes upon his grave!

"The love you bore to him found a responsive pulse-beat in his generous heart. As he gave you love, so in return has asked of you in life, and asks of you dead, nothing but love. This passionate devotion to his people was well exemplified by his last utterance on his saintly deathbed: again and again to watchers by his couch of death, in the long stillness of the night and through the dreary stretches of the winter day, he murmured, 'I am going home, do not forget me'.

"So long as human hearts beat fondly for justice, charity and sacrifice, will the name and fame of Fr. Garin be cherished by the citizens of Lowell as a rich inheritance, and then by the Catholics of our city as a special legacy.

"He has gone home; we shall not forget him."

Finally, as reported in The Star: "It was an occasion the solemnity of which seldom has been equaled in Lowell. Never did the streets present such a sight. They were crowded from early morning, and no one even if unacquainted with the circumstances could have mistaken the occasion for one of joy instead of sorrow.

"Sad were the faces and hushed the voices of the people who were waiting uncomplainingly for hours in the chill atmosphere to do a last reverence to Father Garin whom they had known only in kindness and merciful ministrations...

"The memory of this good man should be kept green and fragrant, as an example and an incentive to all who come after him.

"The Star ventures to express the hope that measures will be taken immediately to start a popular subscription for the erection of a statue to be placed near the St. Jean Baptiste church and which may forever preserve the lineaments of the features which have become so dear to many thousands of people.

"Who has done more for the best interests of Lowell? Who has had the wisdom given him to lead a people for more than a quarter century, which beginning with 1,200 obscure individuals has become so compact a body of 20,000 progressive, enterprising, respected citizens of our great municipality? Such a movement should receive the sympathy and the substantial support of every citizen whose soul is broad enough to comprehend the elements of true greatness."[8]

The wish of the Star rapidly took shape. A citizens' committee was organized under the direction of Father Dioscoride Forget, and quickly set to work. They retained the services of Canadian sculptor Louis Philippe

Hebert, well known for his previous accomplishments. The project advanced rapidly, and the statue was cast in the Henry Bunnard foundry of New York. The people of Lowell began waiting impatiently for the day of the unveiling. L'Etoile, the French language paper, seemed to increase the excitement by referring to it often. We may say that the entire population contributed to the erection of that monument to the honor of the "Bon Pere", since the money poured in not only from the Canadians and the Catholics, but from everyone high and low. An enthusiastic populace raised all the necessary funds in only one month and a half.[9]

On October 22, 1896, at an elaborate church ceremony, Father Garin's great character was once again brought to light. Outdoors, the civil celebration followed, with the entire population participating in this new triumph. The Lowell Evening Mail[10] described the event thus: "Never in the history of the city was such a mass of people seen in that section of the city. The street was packed solid with people from early in the evening and long before the time for the unveiling of the statue the street was thronged with such an impregnable mass and the running of street cars was out of the question altogether..."

The newspaper then quotes from a speech given by J.H. Guillet the chairman of the committee: "The people of Lowell, regardless of religious preference and true to their spirit of fairness and liberality desiring to pay a just tribute of esteem and gratitude to the memory of Rev. Father Garin, have caused this statue to be erected near this beautiful church, his last work among us."

Lowell's mayor, Mr. W.F. Courtney, spoke the following words: "It is seldom that a man is fully appreciated during his lifetime. His fellow men are usually so intent upon their own personal affairs that they seldom take time to consider the greatness and the kindness of those who live around them...Father Garin...was the Moses who led our French-Canadian brethren out of the wilderness and taught them to appreciate the laws and institution of our country and to become patriotic American citizens...This beautiful statue which is an ornament in our city, was not erected alone by the Franco-Canadian brethren, nor by the Catholics of our city, but by the citizens of Lowell, without regard to race or creed."

Finally, Mr. Charles Palmer, a former mayor, added to the praise: "When well meaning but injudicious zealots sought to bring religious controversy into our municipal affairs and to stir up sectarian strife from which our city has been happily free, Father Garin was the first to rebuke them. 'I will never' he said to me later, 'countenance the introduction of sectarian issues into our government. This country is and must remain the home of religious freedom. The Catholics of Lowell will give you no trouble Mr. Mayor. We will fight evil, not one another.'"

Every superior of the Oblate province of Canada made it a point to attend this ceremony in honor of their colleague. When Archbishop Thomas Duhamel of Ottawa pulled the string that unveiled the statue, everyone beheld Father Garin in his favorite stance, one hand pointing forward, as if instructing his people, and the other grasping the plan of his beloved St. Jean-Baptiste Church. The engraving on the pedestal summarizes his life in a few words, and gives us the reason for this monument.

REV. A. GARIN, OMI
BORN IN FRANCE, MAY 7, 1822
DIED IN LOWELL, FEB. 16, 1895
HE WENT ABOUT DOING GOOD
ERECTED BY THE PEOPLE OF LOWELL

Father Garin was thus raised to the ranks of the immortals.

ADDENDUM:

The spirit of service which Father Garin's pioneering community brought to Lowell continues very strongly today in the Shrine of St. Joseph the Worker, the parishes of the Immaculate Conception, Ste. Jeanne d'Arc, Sacred Heart, Notre Dame de Lourdes, Ste. Marie, St. William, and Nuestra Senora del Carmen. It lives on in the chaplaincies at Saints Memorial, St. Joseph, and the Tewksbury State Hospitals, as well as in several collaborative ministries in search of peace and justice. Young men and women from the Lowell Oblate parishes are serving as missionaries in all parts of the world.

Due to contemporary upward mobility, the large number of Franco-American families who once lived in the environs of St. Jean-Baptiste church are now living their Faith in the suburbs or in other parts of the country. The reduced number who remain in this area are no longer able to maintain this beautiful structure as befits a house of worship. To everyone's regret the parish had to be dissolved in 1993 after 125 years of existence. The occasion was marked with a joyous but nostalgic celebration in thanksgiving for the blessings that had touched so many parishioners and friends in past years. Wistfully, the doors were closed, but not for long.

In recent years several different groups of Hispanics have been attracted to Lowell. A central church was needed for all of them to practice their common Faith. The Oblates of Mary Immaculate have a long tradition of ministering in Spanish. Since the Hispanics were now large enough as a unified group to take upon themselves the responsibility for this church, a new parish was formed, under the patronage of Nuestra Senora del Carmen. Today Spanish hymns resonate with gusto in the rejuvenated interior. The church that Father Garin began in the pioneering days of the French speaking minority is again serving spiritual needs, this time for Spanish speaking immigrants.

The true missionary spirit of Father Garin lives on in Lowell. Through his accomplishments, faith in a better humanity continues to thrive. His dynamic spirit began to show itself with the native Americans of northern and eastern Canada, came to its highest point when he took the city of Lowell to task, and continues today in the shadow of his statue, through the services of the Oblate Fathers to the Hispanic community in the same city.

Lucien A. Sawyer OMI

THE MAN LOWELL REMEMBERED

Footnotes — Chapter One

[1]Philibert Garin and his wife had six children: Paul Leonard (2 November 1813), Andre Felicien (11 June 1817), Josephine (27 June 1818), Claude (2 August 1819), Louis (2 January 1821) and Andre Marie. (Notes graciously furnished by M. V. Chomel, curator, Archives Department of the Isere, Grenoble.)

[2]Jean IMBERT, Histoire de la Cote-Saint-Andre, The Cote-Saint-Andre, Marmonnier, 1944, p. 29.

[3]Ibid., p. 53.

[4]Ibid., p. 10.

[5]The baptismal document states: "Andre GARIN, legitimate son of 'Sieur' Philibert and of Françoise EMPTOZ-FALCOZ, born yesterday, was baptized on May 10, 1822. Andre EMPTOZ-FALCOZ was his godfather, and Thérèse MEYNIER, his godmother. "Signed: DURAND, Pastor." (Note furnished by Abbe Louis Vannier, Pastor, Archpriest of Cote-Saint-Andre, September 1, 1959.) The civic document is more detailed: "No. 60 -- on Friday, May 10, 1822, at nine o'clock in the morning, this document records the birth of Andre Garin, born yesterday at seven o'clock in the evening, the natural and legitimate son of 'Sieur' Philibert GUARIN, merchant-grocer, domiciled at Cote-Saint-Andre and of Françoise EMPTOZ-FALCOZ, married. The infant was a male. First witness, Mr. Andre REVERCHON, innkeeper, 28 years old, second witness Mr. Joseph FAVRE, shoemaker, 23 years old, both domiciled at Cote-Saint-Andre, at the request made to me by 'Sieur' Philibert GUARIN, father of the infant and signed by all after reading the present document. P. GARIN REVER-CHON FAVRE "Certified by me, Jules BUISSON, assistant to the mayor of the Côte Saint Andre and public officer of the state. Buisson, Assistant." (Information furnished by M. V. Chomel.)

[6]As the result of an 1810 agreement between the local city and the Bishop of Grenoble, a minor seminary-college was established in the former convent of the Franciscan Recollets. Under the guidance of the directors, the Abbes Douillet, Mermet and Mollard, many "Brothers of Mary" were trained in this establishment and the Marist Brothers took over in 1846 (J. Imbert, op cit., pp 209-210). It was later demolished to build a

splendid seminary, which was taken over by the government in 1906 and turned into a departmental orphanage.

[7]Ibid., op. cit., pp 261-262.

[8]Notices Necrologiques, OMI (Obituary Notices from the Oblates of Mary Immaculate), vol. 7, p. 406. The title of "Sieur" that preceded the name of Philibert Garin in the baptismal record and the description of "merchant-grocer" found in the civil documents indicate that Philibert Garin was a man of some wealth.

[9]Notices Necrologiques, vol. 7, p. 406.

[10]Chronicles of the Sisters of the Holy Names of Jesus and Mary, and Souvenir des noces d'or religieuses du R.P. Andre-Marie Garin, OMI Lowell, Mass., Impr. du National, pp 87-88.

[11]The Oblates of Mary Immaculate had established their Novitiate there on February 17, 1841 (Missions des Oblats de Marie Immaculee) 30 (1892), p. 418).

[12]Notices Necrologiques, vol. 1, p. 227 (notice of Father Auguste Albert Brunet).

[13]Notices Necrologiques, vol. 3, p. 214 (accounts from Father Charles Baret).

[14]Testimonial of the Golden Anniversary, (Souvenir des noces d'or...) pp 88-90.

[15]According to other sources, Father Garin completed his studies in philosophy at the Seminary of Grenoble before entering the Novitiate.

[16]Notices Necrologiques, vol. 7, pp 407-408.

[17]The street was thus named because a confraternity of men attired in red robes worshiped at the chapel located there. (Augustine FABRE, Le rues de Marseille. This information about the seminary of Marseilles was graciously furnished by Father Charles Sety, OMI, from the Aix-en-Provence community.

[18]Notices Necrologiques, vol. 1, p. 29 (notes of Father Charles Bellon).

[19]The scholastics were not separated from the seminarians until 1852, when they were installed at Mount Olivet (Marseilles). Missions, 14 (1876) p. 114.

[20]Testimonial of the Golden Anniversary, p. 11.

[21]Bishop de Mazenod wrote in his journal, February 17, 1844: "Young Fabre, the finest student at the seminary, has been admitted as a novice."

²²It would seem, however, that in the founder's mind, Brother Garin had already been destined to Canada for some time, since on August 17, 1843, Bishop de Mazenod entered in his journal: "Mass at Notre Dame de la Garde. As usual, went to the Shrine on the Thursday within the octave of the feast, and announced the miracle performed by the Blessed Virgin in favor of Sister Marie Julie Dugas, religious of the Holy Monastery of the Visitation. I had young Oblates to accompany me, Brothers Brunet, Garin, and Laverlochere, who entrusted themselves and their mission to our good Mother...One cannot harbor worthier feelings for one's vocation. They are leaving for Canada." (Yenveux Manuscript I, 102 (52).) See also his letter to Father Aubert, May 4,1844.

Footnotes — Chapter Two

¹Missions OMI, 25 (1887), p. 69. On June 11, 1844, Bishop de Mazenod wrote in his diary: "The departure of Father Guigues and of Brother Garin, deacon, for Canada." (Yenveux Manuscript, VII, 114 (86).

²December 2, 1841.

³Codex Historicus de Longueuil, p. 40. (Montreal archives) Typewritten copy.

⁴Fidelis, Mere Marie-Rose, Montreal, Desbarats & Cie, 1985, p. 330.

⁵Allard to Tempier, January 21, 1845 (OMI General Archives, Allard records).

⁶Fidelis, op. cit., p. 330.

⁷Pierre Duchaussois, OMI, Rose du Canada, Montreal, Granger Freres, 1932, p. 162.

⁸Codex Historicus de Longueuil, p. 48.

⁹Registre des Lettres, vol. 3, p. 432 (Archdiocese of Montreal). The Founder held Brother Garin in high esteem, since he wrote to Father Honorat on June 8, 1844: "I have left Father Guigues with our Father Pierre Aubert and Brother Garin, the charming Oblate who is still a deacon, but who will be very useful to the mission. It cannot be said we are lacking in generosity. The three members left without regard for human emotions. They all sacrificed Europe without even saying good-bye to their families. One sees these traits in some other Orders. I am happy to

see that we also can practice the noblest virtues."
(<u>Yenveux Manuscript</u>, I, 94 (47)).

Footnotes — Chapter Three

[1]<u>Notices Necrologiques</u>, vol. 7, p. 410. On Father Laverlochere, see Gaston Carriere, OMI, <u>Missionnaire sans toit</u>, Montreal, Rayonnement, 1963.

[2]This shrine must have reminded him of his visits to Notre Dame de l'Osier and to Notre Dame de la Garde in Marseilles.

[3]To a colleague, 10 December 1853, in <u>Rapport ... de la Propagation de la Foi...de Montreal</u>, 1853-1854, p. 83.

[4]<u>Rapport sur les missions du diocese de Quebec</u>, 1845 p.119. Letter dated August 25, 1845.

[5]<u>Ibidem</u>, 1845, pp 126-127.

[6]OMI General Archives, Guigues record.

[7]<u>Notices Necrologiques</u>, vol. 7, p. 410.

[8]<u>Codex Historicus de Longueuil</u>, p. 77.

[9]<u>Rapport sur les Missions du diocese de Quebec</u>, 1853. p. 137. This account is perfectly correct; see Gaston Carriere, OMI, <u>Les Missions catholiques dans l'Est du Canada et l'Honorable Compagnie de la Baie d'Hudson</u>, (1844-1900), Ottawa, University Editions, 1957, p. 83 ff.

[10]<u>Codex Historicus de Longueuil</u>, p. 81.

[11]<u>Ibidem</u>, pp 82-83.

[12]The residence of Fort Albany was established in 1892.

[13]To a colleague, in <u>Rapport sur les Missions du diocese de Quebec</u>,1853, p. 4 and 13.

[14]<u>Rapport de...la Propagation de la Foi...de Montreal</u>, 1853, p. 148.

[15]Father Garin's travels frequently occurred in the company of the Protestant minister, a source of some difficulties. See Gaston Carriere, OMI, <u>Les missions catholiques</u>... p. 67-68.

[16]Aubert to Vandenberghe, May 10, 1870 (Provincial Archives, General Administration record).

[1]Codex Historicus de Longueuil, p. 97 and Notices Necrologiques, Vol. 7 p. 410.

[2]Testimonial of the Golden Anniversary, p. 30.

[3] Regarding Father Arnaud, see Gaston Carriere, OMI, Le Roi de Betsiamites (The King of Betsiamites), Ottawa, University Editions, 1958.

[4]Regarding Father Durocher, see Gaston CARRIERE, OMI, Un Apotre a Quebec, le pere Flavien Durocher OMI, Montreal, Rayonnement, 1960.

[5]To the Archbishop of Quebec, July 26, 1846, in Rapport sur les Missions du diocese de Quebec, 1847, p. 113.

[6]Ibidem, p. 114.

[7]Durocher to the Archbishop, July 6, 1846 (Archdiocese of Quebec record P.P.O. I-50, 51) p. 123.

[8]They arrived there October 8, 1846 (Durocher to Cazeau, October 8, 1846; Provincial Archives, OMI, Durocher record).

[9]Notices Necrologiques, vol. 3, p. 28.

[10]October 30, 1846 (OMI Provincial Archives, F. Durocher record).

[11]August 1, 1847, in Codex Historicus de Longueuil, pp 93-96.

[12]Diocese of Chicoutimi, Series XVII, parish 9, no. 5, vol 3, p. 28.

[13]Arnaud to Guigues, November 10, 1850 (OMI Provincial Archives).

[14]Notices Necrologiques, vol. 7, p. 411.

[15]Registre des depenses, de l'Eglise St. Pierre de Montreal, p. 2 (OMI Provincial Archives, Montreal); Missions OMI, 30 (1892), p. 59.

[16]Codex Historicus de Montreal, p. 127.

[17]Ibidem, pp 118-123.

[18]February 2 - 23 (ibid., pp 123-125).

[19]Ibid., pp 125-126.

[20]Notices Necrologiques, vol. 7, p. 412.

[21]J.M.R. Villeneuve, OMI, Notes manuscrites sur la province du Canada, p. 30, (Deschatelets Archives) - Father Baveux was known in Canada by the name of Leonard.

[1]Today known as Cooperville, New York. See <u>Codex Historicus de Longueuil</u>, p.143.

[2]J. S. Michaud. "The diocese of Burlington", in <u>History of the Catholic Church in New England States</u>, Boston, The Hud & Everts Co., 1899, vol. 2. p. 566.

[3]<u>Registre des Lettres</u>, vol. 8, p. 254.

[4]Report of Father F. Vandenberghe, in <u>Missions OMI</u>, 8 (1869), p. 312.

[5]Page 100 (Deschâtelets Archives, Saint Joseph Scholasticate, Ottawa).

[6]<u>Registre des Lettres</u>, vol. 8, p. 254.

[7]The cost went up, on May 8, 1861, to $8,756.46 (<u>actes officiels</u>, p.154).

[8]Annals of the Gray Nuns.

[9]To Guigues, September 4, 1860 (OMI Provincial Archives, Plattsburgh record).

[10]Page 43.

[11]June 1, 1860.

[12]<u>Correspondence</u>, vol. 1, p. 118.

[13]<u>Registre des Lettres</u>, vol. 8, p. 262.

[14](<u>Registre des Lettres</u>, vol. 6, p.325) October 26, 1856.

[15]Lowell <u>L'Etoile</u>, Memorial issue, March 1895.

[16]Registre des Lettres, vol. 9, pp 248 ff. On September 30 1862, Bishop Guigues wrote to Father Fabre that Father Garin could replace Father Chevalier (<u>Correspondence</u>, vol. 1, p. 221).

[17]OMI Provincial Archives, Buffalo record.

[18]<u>Ibidem</u>.

[19]OMI General Archives, Guigues record.

[20]January 25, 1863 (<u>ibidem</u>, Garin record).

[21]OMI General Archives, Guigues record.

[22]<u>Ibidem</u>, Garin record.

[23]April 13, 1864 (<u>Correspondence</u>, vol. 1, p. 236).

[24]September 30 (OMI General Archives, Garin record).

[25]<u>Correspondence</u>, vol. 1, p. 224.

[26]<u>Ibidem</u>, vol. 1, p. 245.

[1]Codex Historicus de Montreal, pp. 216-217

[2]OMI General Archives, Vandenberghe records.

[3]OMI Provincial Archives, General Administration records.

[4]December 23.

[5]OMI Provincial Archives, Boston record.

[6]Archdiocese of Boston, document no. 15.

[7]OMI Provincial Archives, General Administration records.

[8]OMI General Archives, Vandenberghe record.

[9]OMI Provincial Archives, Boston record.

[10]March 19, 1868 (OMI General Archives, Vandenberghe records).

[11]According to Mr. Albert Bergeron, the priests lived for some time at the home of his grandfather, Mr. Louis Bergeron, on Cabot Street. This stay must have been of very short duration because the missionaries were the guests of St. Patrick's pastor.

[12]OMI Provincial Archives, Boston record.

[13]Ibidem.

[14]Ibidem.

[15] See James S. Sullivan, One Hundred Years of Progress, A Graphic, Historical, and Pictorial Account of the Catholic Church in New England, Boston and Portland, Illustrated Publishing Company, 1895, p. 304.

[16]This action of Father Garin is the one Father Lagier complained about in his first letter.

[17]J. S. Sullivan, loc. cit., p. 305.

[18]Missions OMI, 23 (1895). pp 106-107.

[19]We can see that Father had trustworthy people among the elder Catholics and even among the "Americans" with whom he shared his projects, so he could count on their sympathy and support.

[20]J. S. Sullivan, p. 305.

[21]OMI Provincial Archives, Boston records.

[22]OMI General Archives, Vandenberghe record.

[23]Correspondence, vol. 1, pp 159-160.

[24]He was not mistaken.

[25]OMI General Archives, Vandenberghe record.

[26]Memoirs Boston diocese, vol. 5, p. 191 (Archdiocese of Boston).

[27] OMI Provincial Archives, Boston records.
[28] _Ibidem._
[29] Archdiocese of Boston.
[30] _Correspondence_, vol. 1, p. 179.
[31] OMI Provincial Archives, Boston records.
[32] J. S. Sullivan _loc. cit._, p. 291.

Footnotes — Chapter Seven

[1] OMI Provincial Archives, Boston record.
[2] Fabre to Vandenberghe, September 17 (OMI Provincial Archives, General Administration record).
[3] OMI Provincial Archives, Boston record
[4] _Ibidem._
[5] OMI Provincial Archives, Lowell record.
[6] _Correspondence_, vol.1, pp 171 and ff.
[7] OMI General Archives, Vandenberghe record.
[8] November 4 (OMI Provincial Archives, General Administration record).
[9] _Ibidem._
[10] OMI Provincial Archives, Lowell record. The meeting had taken place October 30.
[11] November 19 (OMI General Archives, Lowell record).
[12] OMI General Archives, Vandenberghe record.
[13] OMI Provincial Archives, Lowell record.
[14] Archdiocese of Boston, Document no. 13.
[15] January 25, 1969 (OMI Provincial Archives, Lowell record). See also J. S. Sullivan _loc. cit._, p. 294.
[16] OMI Provincial Archives, Lowell record.
[17] Archdiocese of Boston, Document no. 21.
[18] OMI General Archives, Vandenberghe record.

Footnotes — Chapter Eight

[1] OMI Provincial Archives, Lowell record.
[2] OMI General Archives, Vandenberghe record.
[3] _Ibidem._

[4]Ibidem.

[5]December 31, 1869 (ibid.).

[6]Garin to the Provincial, May 31, 1870 (OMI Provincial Archives, Lowell record).

[7]Vandenberghe to Fabre, July 22, 1870 (OMI General Archives, Vandenberghe record).

[8]J. S. Sullivan loc cit., p. 295.

[9]Vandenberghe to Fabre, December 16, 1870 (OMI General Archives, Vandenberghe record).

[10]Ibidem.

[11]OMI Provincial Archives, Lowell record.

[12]Ibidem.

[13]Father Garin wrote on the 15th and the Provincial replied on the 17th (Correspondence, vol. 2, p. 226).

[14]OMI General Archives, Vandenberghe record.

[15]To Fabre, August 10, 1871 (ibidem).

[16]Garin to Vandenberghe, April 27 (OMI Provincial Archives, Lowell record).

[17]Ibidem.

[18]OMI General Archives, Vandenberghe record.

[19]Ibidem.

[20]J. S. Sullivan, loc. cit., p. 297.

[21]OMI Provincial Archives, Lowell record.

[22]OMI General Archives, Vandenberghe record.

[23]January 15, 1872 (OMI Provincial Archives, General Administration record).

[24]February 10th (OMI General Archives, Vandenberghe record).

[25]Episcopal Register, July 7, 1872 (Archdiocese of Boston).

[26]OMI General Archives, Mangin record.

[27]To Fabre, June 10, 1877 (OMI General Archives, Antoine record).

[28]Notices Necrologiquyes, vol. 7, p. 416.

[29]Missions OMI, 15 (1877), pp 463-472.

[30]OMI General Archives, Garin record.

[31]November 14.

[1]To the Provincial, May 1, 1869 (OMI Provincial Archives, Lowell records).

[2]To the Provincial, October 28 (ibidem).

[3]To the Provincial, February 22 (ibidem).

[4]The parish reported 2,400 communicants.

[5]J. S. Sullivan, loc cit., p. 307.

[6]To the Provincial, November 29, 1877 (OMI Provincial Archives, Lowell records).

[7]J. S. Sullivan, loc cit., p. 307.

[8]September 11, 1880 (OMI Provincial Archives, Lowell records).

[9]Episcopal Register, May 21, 1884 (Archdiocese of Boston).

[10]J. S. Sullivan, loc cit., p. 307, and J. McGrath, OMI, in Missions OMI, 20 (1882), p. 13.

[11]OMI Provincial Archives, Lowell records.

[12]As of 1888, he had purchased property adjacent to the rectory from the Tremont & Suffolk Company.

[13]Codex Historicus of the St. Joseph Residence p. 21.

[14]OMI General Archives, Garin records.

[15]Father would sell stones through the children, and they would be responsible for keeping a record of each donor.

[16]It cost $30,000.

[17]Episcopal Register (Archdiocese of Boston).

[18]OMI General Archives, Garin record. Father Garin continued offering Mass in St. Joseph's Church until his death.

[19]July 15, 1893 (ibidem).

[20]Episcopal Register (loc. cit.).

[21]Father Bullard, OMI, in Missions OMI, 46 (1908), pp 311-312. The church towers were never built.

[22]Ibid., p. 322. St. Jeanne d'Arc Parish was established in 1922. In 1947, St. Joseph Parish took the name of St. Jean-Baptiste and the old church became a shrine on May 10, 1956.

[23]Album souvenir et historique de la paroisse Saint-Joseph de Lowell, Mass., 1916, p. 84.

[24]Antoine Clement, in L'Etoile, October 24, 1936, p. 46.

[25]Ibidem.

[26]There was also a St. Andre section of the Catholic Foresters.

[27]On Sunday, Father Garin never missed singing in his beautiful voice during vespers. He was always very active in ministry as evidenced by the records. His first church service took place on May 3, 1868, and his last, on November 24, 1894.

[28]OMI General Archives, Garin records.

[29]Fournier to the Provincial, March 23, 1876 (OMI Provincial Archives, Lowell records).

[30]November 1, 1881, in Missions OMI, 20 (1882), p. 13.

[31]To the Provincial, January 12, 1881 (OMI Provincial Archives, Lowell records).

[32]McGrath to the Provincial, June 5 (ibidem).

[33]OMI Provincial Archives, Lowell records.

[34]Ibidem.

[35]Ibidem.

[36]J. S. Sullivan, loc cit., p. 307; Missions OMI, 46 (1908), p. 307 and Berthe Desmarais, in L'Etoile, October 24, 1936, p. 17.

[37]Codex Historicus of St. Joseph Residence p. 17.

[38]Missions OMI, 46 (1908), p. 307. We read that Father Garin often visited the classrooms and on the feast of Saint Andre there were great demonstrations in his honor.

[39]Notes of Sister Paul-Emile, S.G.C.

[40]Missions OMI, 23 (1885), p. 120.

[41]OMI General Archives, Garin records.

[42]June 20, 1890 (ibidem).

[43]Codex Historicus of St. Joseph Residence p. 25.

[44]Ibidem.

[45]OMI General Archives, Garin records.

[46]Codex Historicus of St. Joseph Residence p. 8.

[47]Missions OMI, 46 (1908), p. 312.

[48]Mangin to Aubert, November 20, 1876 (OMI General Archives, Mangin records).

[49]It seems that on the first evening spent in the St. Joseph Residence they sang and amused themselves far into the night.

[1]OMI Provincial Archives, Lowell records.

[2]Mission OMI, 20 (1881), p. 117.

[3]Notices Necrologiques, vol. 7. pp 415-416. Father Garin, known as the Father of the Canadians, was sent one day to Fall River where difficulties arose between the parish priest and the parishioners. When he was introduced to the people, they asked him bluntly: "Are you 'canayen' like us or like the French?" Without loosing his composure, the Father promptly replied, "Like all of you." His answer released a thunderous applause, his mission was a success.

[4]November 6, 1871 (OMI Provincial Archives, Lowell records.)

[5]Ibidem.

[6]November 8, 1871 (ibidem).

[7]November 20, 1871 (ibidem).

[8]Archdiocese of Quebec.

[9]To the Provincial, July 14, 1872 (OMI Provincial Archives, Lowell records). See also Vandenberghe to Fabre, July 16, 1872 (OMI General Archives, Vandenberghe records).

[10]James S. Sullivan, loc cit., p. 398. See also R.H. Lord, History of the Diocese of Boston, New York, Sheed & Ward, 1944, vol. 2, p. 207.

[11]They had bought the church from the Orthodox Society of Billerica. The first Mass was celebrated by Father Garin (Lowell Daily News, October 20, 1893).

[12]OMI General Archives, Vandenberghe records.

[13]Tortel to Fabre, November 14, 1883 (ibidem, Tortel records). See also J. S. Sullivan, loc cit., p. 361.

[14]Missions OMI, 55 (1921), p. 373.

[15]OMI General Archives, Tabaret records.

[16]Louis Gladu to the Provincial, September 26, 1884 (Ibidem, Gladu records).

¹Archives of the Gray Sisters of the Cross, Ottawa, Bruyere record, doc. 377.

²Ibidem, doc. 378.

³Ibidem.

⁴Pages 49-50.

⁵Missions OMI, 46 (1908), p. 306.

⁶Notices Necologiques,vol. 7, p. 427.

⁷OMI General Archives, Visit: Lowell records.

⁸His sermons were to the point and delivered in a resonant voice. At home people would sometimes say, "That was a powerful one today."

⁹It has been said: "For some years, there existed an avant-garde group who would have desired to put a curb on the activities of the priest, by opening a very liberal bookstore, organizing dances, and inviting people to fun gatherings. Fortunately, Father Garin was able to check these tendencies and prevent the dances. The group eventually shrank to four." (Album Souvenir et Historique...,p. 8). It was under Father Garin that Father Geny initiated the work of "La Bonne Presse," a lending library at Saint Joseph's Church, in 1893.

¹⁰Notices Necrologiques, vol. 7, p. 414-415.

¹¹Missions OMI, 52 (1914), p. 165.

¹²L'Apostolat des Oblats... (Lowell Edition), 1943, p. 39.

¹³November 24, 1876 (OMI General Archives, Garin records).

¹⁴Souvenir des noces d'or..., p. 11.

¹⁵November 18, 1892 (OMI General Archives, Garin records).

¹⁶The priest was returning from the General Chapter and a visit with his family.

¹⁷July 15, 1893 (OMI General Archives, Garin records).

¹⁸To Fabre, February 2, 1871 (OMI General Archives, Vandenberghe).

¹⁹Ibidem, Garin records.

²⁰Missions OMI, 23 (1885), p. 108.

²¹Ibidem, p. 109-110.

²²L'Etoile, Souvenir Issue, March 1895. The veneration lavished on the Father was such that, after his death, almost all the families kept statuettes modeled on the monument erected in his honor.

²³On his return from Europe in 1893, the parishioners said with a chuckle: "Our Father is still wearing his same old hat."

²⁴Notices Necrologiques, vol. 7, pp 419-420.

[1]<u>Missions OMI,</u> 30 (1892), p. 401.

[2]The visitor was the Rev. A. Saint John Chambre, of Saint Anne's Episcopalian Church.

[3]<u>Missions OMI</u>, 33 (1895), p. 270.

[4]February 16, 1895.

[5]March 11, 1895.

[6]"Ecclesiastes", 9, 14-18.

[7]Mr. Farley was not familiar with the Indian tribes of Canada. Father Garin never dealt with the Iroquois.

[8]February 19, 1895.

[9]<u>Lowell Evening Mail</u>, October 22, 1896.

[10]<u>Ibidem.</u>

BIBLIOGRAPHY

Albert, Felix, <u>Immigrant Odyssey, A French Canadian Habita</u>
<u>New England,</u> Translation by Arthur L. Eno, Jr., Orono M(
University of Maine Press, 1993.

<u>Album-Souvenir et Historique de la paroisse Saint Joseph de</u>
<u>Mass.,</u> Lowell, Imprimerie de l'Etoile, 1915.

Brault, Gerard J., <u>The French Canadian Heritage in New Engl</u>
Hanover NH, University Press of New England, 1986.

Carriere, Gaston OMI, <u>Le pere Louis Etienne Reboul,</u> Ottawa
University Editions, 1959.

_____, <u>Le roi des Betsiamites,</u> Ottawa, University Editions,

_____, <u>Les Missions Catholiques dans l'est du Canada et l'</u>
<u>Compagnie de la Baie d'Hudson</u> (<u>1844-1900</u>), Ottawa, Univ
Editions, 1957.

_____, <u>Missionnaire sans toit,</u> Montreal, Rayonnement, 196.

_____, <u>Un apotre a Quebec, le pere Flavien Durocher OMI,</u>
Rayonnement, 1960.

Duchaussois, Pierre OMI, <u>Rose du Canada,</u> Montreal, Granger
1932.

Eno, Arthur L. Jr., Editor, <u>Cotton was King, A History of Lowe</u>
<u>Massachusetts,</u> New Hampshire Publising Company and th
Historical Society, 1976.

Fidelis, <u>Mere Marie Rose,</u> Montreal, Desbarats & Cie., 1895.

Gagnon, Herve OMI, <u>It All Began in 1868 . . . (Spring Festival</u>
Lowell, MA, St. Joseph the Worker Shrine, 1993.

Hendrickson, Dyke, <u>Quiet Presence, Histoires de Franco-Amer</u>
<u>New England,</u> Portland ME, Guy Gannett, 1980.

Imbert, Jean, <u>Histoire de la Cote St. Andre,</u> Marmonier, 1944.

L'Etoile, Memorial Issue, Lowell, MA March, 1895.

Lord, R.H., History of the Archdiocese of Boston, New York, Sheed and Ward, 1944.

Michaud, J.S., History of the Catholic Church in New England States, Boston, Hud and Everts Company, 1899.

National Park Service, Lowell, The Story of an Industrial City, Washington, DC,. Department of the Interior, 1992.

O'Toole, James M., Guide to the Archives of the Archdiocese of Boston, New York, Garland and Company, 1982.

Paul-Emile, Soeur SGC, Amiskwaski, La terre du castor, Ottawa, University Editions, 1952.

Quintal, Claire, The Little Canadas of New England, Worcester MA, French Institute/Assumption College, 1983.

Santerre, Richard, La paroisse Saint-Jean Baptiste et les Franco-Americains de Lowell, Massachusetts, Manchester NH, Editions Lafayette, 1993.

_____, The Franco-Americans of Lowell, Massachusetts, Lowell, MA, The Franco-American Day Committee, 1972.

Sawyer, Lucien OMI and Ouellette, Paul OMI, History of St. Joseph Cemetery, 1894-1994, Chelmsford, MA Privately Printed, 1994.

Souvenir des noces d'or religieuses du R.P. Andre-Marie Garin OMI, Lowell MA, Imprim. du National, 1892.

Sullivan, James S. One Hundred Years of Progress, A Graphic, Historical, and Pictorial Account of the Catholic Church in New England, Boston MA and Portland ME, Illustrated Publishing Company, 1895.

Wilde, Joseph C. OMI, Men of Hope, The Backgroud and History of the Oblate Province of Our Lady of Hope (Eastern Province of the Missionary Oblates of Mary Immaculate). Washington DC, Oblate Fathers, 1967.